GROWING HERBS

FROM SEED, CUTTING & ROOT

GROWING HERBS

FROM SEED, CUTTING & ROOT

AN ADVENTURE IN SMALL MIRACLES

THOMAS DeBAGGIO

Introduction by Jim Wilson of *The Victory Garden*

INTERWEAVE PRESS

Growing Herbs from Seed, Cutting and Root
An Adventure in Small Miracles
By Thomas DeBaggio
With Foreword by Jim Wilson

Photography: Joe Coca unless otherwise noted
Production: Dean Howes

Interweave, Inc.
201 East Fourth Street
Loveland, Colorado 80537
USA

Printed in China by Midas Printing International

Library of Congress Cataloging-in-Publication Data

DeBaggio, Thomas, 1942-
    Growing herbs from seed, cutting and root: an adventure in small miracles/by
    Thomas DeBaggio; with foreword by Jim Wilson.
        p. cm.
Revised.
Includes bibliographical references (p.).
ISBN 1-883010-78-0
    1. Herb—Propagation. 2. Herb gardening. I. Title.

SB351.H5 D43 2000
635'.7—dc21   00-027580

First Printing: IWP—5M:400:CC

To my son, Francesco,
who sacrificed the best afternoons of his youth
so I could pursue my dream to grow herbs
on what he thought would be his backyard soccer field.

FOREWORD

I met Tom and Joyce DeBaggio several years ago when my wife and I traveled to Washington, DC, for the first International Master Gardening Conference. For a few years, we had been growing herbs for cutting and shipping to fine restaurants all over the country. We had heard that Tom knew a lot about growing and using culinary herbs and wanted to compare our experiences. Commercial herb growers were few and far between during those years.

Well, the word about Tom's know-how was, if anything, understated. Did he know herbs! We went to an excellent Greek restaurant near their home in Arlington and talked all the way through dinner. I think we did justice to the excellent food, but what I remember most vividly were the many life experiences Tom shared with us. He comes about as close to being a "Renaissance Man" as anyone I know, and his ties to the "old country" have given him a unique appreciation of the subtle differences among the many cultivars within each species of herb. (I must confess that, while I can tell the difference between the aroma and flavor of lemon, cinnamon, and common sweet basil, I can't distinguish common basil from the reportedly more flavorful varieties such as 'Genoa Green Improved.')

Tom didn't start out as a horticulturist. His formal education was in journalism, and it shows in the imaginative but honest descriptions of herbs in his catalog. Yet, his most meaningful education began years ago when he decided to ride the wave of public interest in herbs that was just gaining speed. He had to learn not only about growing herbs under garden conditions but how to propagate them efficiently. This meant building greenhouses, one after another, until his city lot in Arlington was virtually roofed with glass. T. DeBaggio Herbs never suffered from a lack of customers; in fact, the problem was too many customers at peak times. Parking space at the Arlington location was restricted, and Tom took seriously his obligation not to allow his business traffic to become a nuisance to his neighbors.

During the years since our first meeting I have crossed paths with Tom at meetings of herbarists here and there. He recently moved his operation to Loudon County, Virginia; his new place is supervised by Tom and his son, Francesco. There Tom has room to produce enough herb plants to meet demand, and where suburban customers can buy them without braving the miserable traffic gridlocks around Washington. My wife and I shut down our herb business after seven years, not because of lack of business, but because I was growing too old to stand up to the heavy work of operating two sizeable greenhouses and three acres of intensively cultivated herbs for cutting and shipping. I went on to become a TV gardener, garden-book writer, and lecturer on several subjects, including herbs.

Over the years, Tom's expertise in herbs continued to grow as he rubbed shoulders with the new breed of chefs around the nation's capital who are developing novel ways to use herbs in cooking, salads, and garnishes. He passes this information on to his customers through his distinctive tabloid-sized catalog.

I like and admire Tom for who he is, for the way he conducts his business, and for his straightforward style of writing. This book, now in its second edition, is an excellent resource for gardeners who need an introduction to growing herbs. I've read it word for word and agree completely with his recommendations for propagating herbs.

I can see you now, leafing through *Growing Herbs from Seed, Cutting and Root*, asking yourself, "How can Tom tell me everything I need to know about growing herbs in this slim book?" Well, he can, and he does. Tom doesn't have an axe to grind. He isn't trying to sell you herb seeds or plants, or supplies for growing them. He doesn't do mail order. He just wants you to succeed on the first try, and that requires knowing which herbs can be started easily from seeds, and which will come true to type only if "cloned" (propagated vegetatively). And Tom wants you to know the soil, sun, and water requirements of each herb species so you won't drown the dryland types and dessicate those that originally hailed from wetland areas.

Tom's long experience in growing many kinds of herbs shines through in his directions. You don't have to know a thing about herbs to let his clear directions flow from your eye to your mind and out your fingertips. Tom, like most senior gardeners, hates to see novices fail or even suffer disappointment. So his directions have undergone revision after revision to remove ambiguities. Yet, amazingly, Tom's zest for growing herbs survived the revisions. It grabs you in the early paragraphs and draws you through page after page. Be forewarned: if you are not already a successful herb gardener, you will be soon. All you have to do is immerse yourself in this book for a few hours, follow the instructions, and you're on your way!

—*Jim Wilson*

PREFACE

This book will tell you, and more important, show you, some of the tricks I've developed for producing large, vigorous, and healthy herbs. I've come by these techniques honestly; I've worked hard for them.

After twenty-five years as a home gardener, I decided two decades ago to grow plants for a living. Herb plants in garden centers, when they could be found then, didn't compare to the gorgeous bedding and vegetable plants by their sides; they had a tragic look to them.

Why didn't herbs look better? The answer was simple: They weren't grown with the same skill and care as bedding plants. There were no books for commercial growers of herbs then, so I began experimenting, and over the years I've come up with a number of innovative ways to grow herb plants.

Thousands of customers and hundreds of thousands of plants have taught me many things about the herb garden. One of the most important lessons I learned early: Gardening isn't only about plants; it's also about time. Contrary to what many gardeners believe, the most important time for a plant is before a seedling germinates or a cutting forms roots.

Seeds await their season of fulfillment, which is unlocked by the gardener who has a clear sense of time.

After the two weeks or so in which a viable seed becomes a healthy, promising seedling (or a thick, vigorous stem-tip becomes a well-rooted cutting), the next most important time is the eight weeks that follow germination or rooting. This is the formative time in the tender world of plants and the most difficult for the home gardener to control, but anybody with some spare space, a little commitment, and the enthusiasm to closely observe nature's unfolding can produce herb transplants to rival a professional's.

While the first ten or twelve weeks in an herb's life are the focus of this book, there are a few tips at the end about transplanting, spacing, and pruning that will get you through the remainder of the season with healthy, bountiful plants.

There are as many reasons to grow your own herbs as there are ways to grow healthy plants, but the main reasons for me are that it's fun, simple, and you get to watch small miracles happen. That's the most satisfying part of herb gardening — next to nibbling a fresh basil leaf in July.

ACKNOWLEDGEMENTS

Behind this book are invaluable friends who helped make its writing easier. My wife, Joyce, offered encouragement, solace, and advice throughout the days and nights of writing, and she protected me from the mental and physical wounds a commercial herb grower suffers during a turbulent and crazy spring. For over thirty years, she has given up much so I could play with words.

Dottie Jacobsen, my chief assistant in the greenhouse, has provided my horticultural endeavors hawk-eyed protection for many years, and I am grateful that her perceptive shield now extends to this literary effort. She also worked diligently and long with two other assistants, Rick Tagg and Laura Schneider, to give me extra time to cultivate words.

My special thanks to Art Tucker of Delaware State University for his willingness, over many years, to share his hard-won knowledge of herbs and for his patient translation of botanical information for a gardener who doesn't know a calyx from a corolla.

Although I'd like to take credit, the idea for this book came from Linda Ligon. Over the many years we've worked together, Linda has wielded her editor's pencil with creative skill and sensitivity. She is the kind of editor about whom writers dream.

This book would be just black and white without Joe Coca, whose brilliance behind the lens created many colorful photos that show more than words can say.

Lyle Craker and Jim Simon supplied helpful advice in person and through their invaluable publication, *The Herb, Spice, and Medicinal Plant Digest,* published by the University of Massachusetts cooperative extension system.

Gary Christensen knows how important he was in the process to get these words between covers; the advice was as good as the lunches.

A garden is an awful responsibility.

You never know what you may be aiding to grow in it.

— Charles Dudley Warner, 1874, My *Summer in a Garden*

CONTENTS

1

i   Foreword by Jim Wilson

iii   Preface

v   Acknowledgements

1   Chapter 1. A Passion for Herbs

7   Chapter 2. Plants From Seed

30   Chapter 3. Plants from Plants

54   Chapter 4. Transplanting and the First Year

61   Chapter 5. Useful Charts

    62   *Chart 1. General Information for Some Common Herbs*
    72   *Chart 2. Herbs Commonly Grown from Seed*
    78   *Chart 3. Herbs Commonly Grown from Cuttings*

84   Spade Work

95   Resources

98   Index

PLANTS FROM SEED

7

PLANTS FROM PLANTS

30

TRANSPLANTING & THE FIRST YEAR

54

With simple tools and a few packets of seed, you can grow herbs in abundance.

A PASSION FOR
HERBS

Like a lot of herb gardeners, I'm often seized with the desire to plant just one more herb, to capture just one more heady aroma from a faraway place. One year, my passion was to possess yet another oregano, as if the more than two dozen types that are grown in the United States weren't enough. I had heard about the quintessential oregano, a tiny-leaved Greek variety that was said to enliven food in a swirl of aroma.

For days, weeks, and months, this elusive plant was on my mind. Then one day a woman stopped in my greenhouse and chanced to recount the story of how her sister had brought just such an oregano to America from their little Greek village. (This was not a miraculous visitation; just another customer.) Greek women, she told me, not only used this oregano for its leaves, they lashed together dried stems to make basting brushes. She said it was a hardy plant: Her sister grew this oregano in Minnesota, where winters are frigid and white. And though its leaves were indeed tiny, she assured me that this oregano wasn't the variety of thyme (*Thymus pulegioides* 'Oregano-scented') which invariably disappoints taste buds that anticipate the real thing. She offered to have her sister bring some seeds to me next time she visited.

A few months after my conversation with this stranger, as Christmas neared, there was a knock on my door. There stood the woman and her sister; they thrust into my hands a plastic bag full of bare, brown stems topped with ripe seeds (I had to take their word that the leaves had been small). I put my nose inside

---

Learning about herbs is both simple and complicated. The aroma of one sometimes mimics that of another, and several herbs may share a common name.

---

the bag and inhaled the delightful fragrance of what I thought would be my long-sought oregano.

I had to know more about this oregano, so I called a botanist friend who has devoted most of his adult life to the study of herbs. He invited me to send him some of the branches and seeds.

A few days after I sent the sample, a short letter arrived from my friend. "Thanks for the summer savory seeds," he said. "Actually, this is not the first time that someone has sent me

Satureja hortensis labeled as oregano. Don't feel too bad."

What a letdown. I always thought the Greeks invented oregano, and now I learn that they don't know the difference between an *Origanum* and a *Satureja*. Summer savory does indeed have small leaves, but it's an annual and temperatures much below freezing kill it. The reason it "came back" each year after Minnesota's deep freeze is that it reseeds itself readily.

The women in the little Greek village and their descendants in America aren't fools, but neither are they botanists. They let their noses and their taste buds teach them what they need to know about herbs, and a misplaced name won't change that.

As my encounter with the small-leaved "Greek oregano" illustrates, learning about herbs is both simple and complicated. The aroma of one sometimes mimics that of another, and several herbs may share a common name. Botanical names can offer more positive identification when they are properly applied, but there is nothing like personal experience with the plants themselves. In the end, it is your nose and your palate that must decide which herb offers the perfect aroma or flavor.

THE AROMA OF HERBS

The aroma of an herb, seemingly so simple and pure, is actually quite complex and

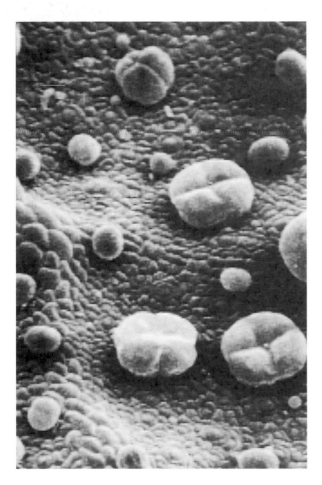

The four-celled head of the basil's fragrance-bearing oil gland can be seen in this 100x magnification.

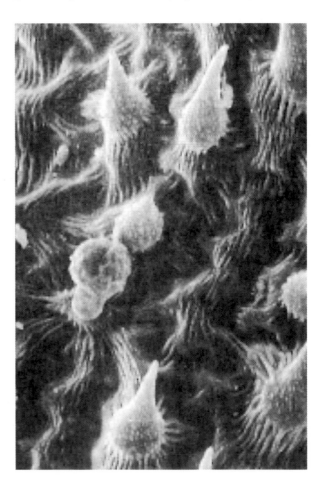

The upper side of a lemon balm leaf at 600x magnification.

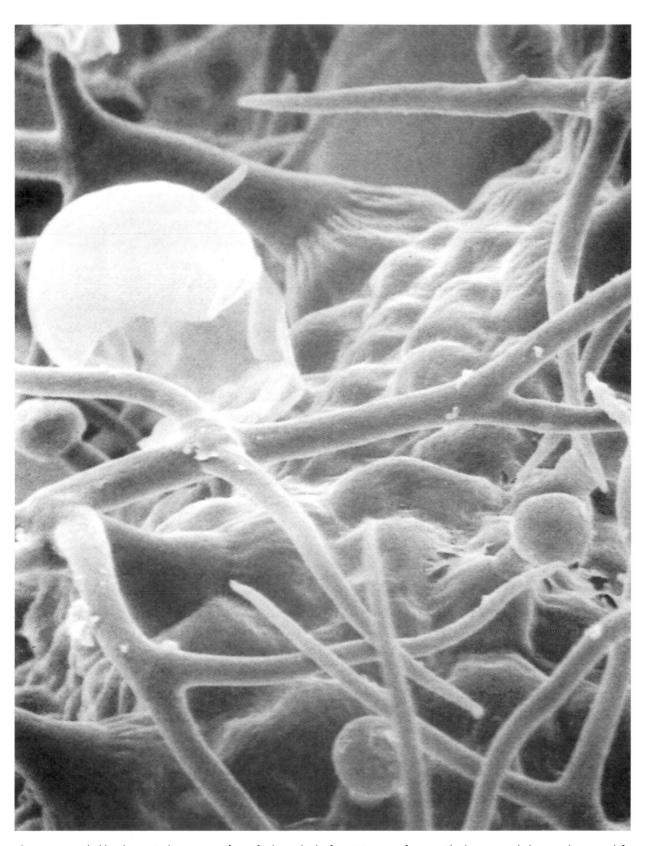

This eerie, tangled landscape is the upper surface of a lavender leaf at 400x magnification. The large round object in the upper left is an oil gland full of the substance that gives the herb its aroma and flavor.

mysterious. Under a microscope or magnifying glass, herb leaves and stems are wondrous landscapes filled with tiny hairs, craters, and mountains — and oil glands that contain the chemicals that produce the herb's particular scent. Minute ruptures in these oil sacs release the aroma when the foliage sways in a breeze or when a hand brushes its leaves.

Scientists aren't certain why plants produce the aromatic chemical soup that gives herbs their aroma and flavor. Do the aromas help in the reproductive process by attracting pollinators, or are they life-preserving repellants? For most of us, the "why" doesn't matter. We love the surprise of sniffing a sage that has a pineapple aroma; we stroke the tiny green leaves of a thyme and marvel that it smells of lemon. We glory in a bed of mint shimmering in the morning sun, giving off scents of oranges, lemons, apples, even lavenders; we bask in the heady, fruity fragrance of sweet Annie and the spicy aroma of the curry plant.

To the gardener, these herb fragrances are exciting and magical; to the scientist with expensive modern equipment, the chemicals that create the fragrances provide liquid fingerprints that can be used, along with traditional botanical methods, to precisely identify plants. These essential oils are quite complex; one recent study of lavender identified more than thirty different chemicals in the fragrance-producing oil. The subtle variations in chemical makeup of similar plants mark important varietal differences and create different aromas. Other herbs have similar numbers of chemicals that work together to produce their fragrances.

To a European of the Mediterranean region, where herbs grow wild and in profusion, the idea of raising herbs in a garden is a bit cockeyed. But if you have only a few square feet of garden in which to seek solace from smog and congestion, as so many in this country do, the allure of all these glorious scents in a garden of one's own is strong.

HOW HERBS REPRODUCE

On those foreign hillsides where wild herbs grow, they reproduce themselves naturally. If you look at the ground carefully on one of those hillsides, you'll see seedlings sprouting and forcing their roots into the rocky soil at the same time they push their heads toward the sun. These plants come from seeds sown freely on the wind by the more mature perennial plants around them or by last year's crop of annuals. A short distance away, another population of plants slowly spreads as the branches that touch the ground sprout roots that dig into the soil and soon become self-sustaining. When branches do this, we call it layering. When the plants' underground roots or rhizomes branch off and send up new plants, we say the plants have spread by their roots. A little farther along our hillside, there is a colony of plants that multiply from their bases; every year each plant has a larger base with more shoots coming from it. We say these herbs multiply from their crowns.

The different ways plants in a natural state increase their population, as well as other ways that require more human intervention, are easily put to use by the resourceful gardener. In the following pages we'll look at these methods in detail.

Hearty starts of pennyroyal, lovage, and Wedgewood English thyme are ready for transplanting into the garden.

Tall and elegant, dill is nonetheless one of the easiest herbs to start from seed.

PLANTS FROM
SEED

Seeds are not dead, dry objects that spring to life; they are instead tender, living organisms at rest. Transforming these specks of dormant vitality into burgeoning plants is one of the great pleasures and challenges open to an herb gardener.

One of the first things you notice about seeds is that even in their smallness there is beauty and complexity. The imperfect roundness of a tawny coriander fruit, etched with thin ribs that give it the illusion of toughness, is brittle; when cracked, it reveals two seeds, both flat on one side and rounded on the other. A basil seed is a quick-change artist: At first it's a hard, black, oblong speck, but once wet, it turns gray-blue, soft, and gelatinous. You can sow thousands of seeds and still find small surprises, such as the day you first realize that the tiny black seeds of onion chives are slightly smaller than those of garlic chives.

Each herb's seed identifies it as surely as its leaf form and fragrance do. The exterior of an herb seed only hints at the world that lies inside it; the seed contains not only a miniature plant, but the idea of the garden.

Even beyond the delightful qualities of form, color, symmetry, and possibility that can be seen and imagined in a seed, there is much that is hidden inside the seed coat until time and germination reveal it. Germination takes place when a living seed absorbs enough water that the tiny organism can begin to use the energy of its stored food; too much or too little water, or soil temperatures too high or too low at this stage, can cause the seed to die. Fortunately, the conditions needed for germination have fairly broad limits; otherwise there would be fewer plants and more frustrated gardeners in the world.

Even beyond the delightful qualities of form, color, symmetry, and possibility that can be seen and imagined in a seed, there is much that is hidden inside the seed coat until time and germination reveal it.

Not all seeds are perfect and alive, so not all in a packet will germinate. A few seed merchants print a germination rate on the packet, but most do not. This information can help you determine how many seeds to sow to produce the number of plants you want, but keep in mind that the seed has been tested under ideal conditions in a laboratory, and the conditions in your backyard garden may differ.

Sometimes there is a reason for the absence of germination information. One year I called a big seed company to ask the germination rate of the sweet woodruff seed it sold. The firm's chief horticulturist told me bluntly that it wasn't known, because the company's staff didn't know how to germinate the seed.

Seeds may germinate poorly for a variety of reasons. Harvest conditions may not have been ideal; seeds on most plants do not ripen simultaneously, and they are usually harvest-

---

Some popular herbs just can't be grown from seed. French tarragon is virtually sterile; it seldom even flowers. Peppermint and Italian oregano (also called hardy marjoram) are hybrids and 99 percent sterile.

---

ed when most seeds are ripe but before the first to ripen begin to scatter. Poor seed-handling techniques after harvest may also contribute to low germination. The seeds of some herbs contain chemicals that inhibit germination until time or environmental conditions remove them; the chemicals sometimes prevent all the seeds from germinating at the same time or at the wrong time. This can be an advantage in nature, where a plant may produce seeds at a time of year when the success of seedlings would be poor.

A germination inhibitor is the reason that

parsley takes so long to germinate. One way to break down the chemical is to place the seeds in old panty hose and soak them for a couple of days in an oxygenated aquarium. This soaking method speeds germination of parsley seed planted in cold ground, but in warmed soil germination improves without this step.

Soil temperature alone also affects the germination of many herb seeds. If it is too low, seeds rot before they sprout, or they germinate poorly. If it is too high, tender embryos die or lie dormant until temperatures decrease. Most herb seeds germinate best when soil temperatures are between 55 and 75°F; the optimum is around 70°F.

Seeds of some herbs must go through a real or simulated cold season before they will germinate. Unless they are left to self-sow outdoors, sweet cicely, echinacea, and angelica seeds should be refrigerated in a plastic bag of moist sphagnum peat moss until they are sown the following spring. Sweet cicely seeds will actually germinate in the refrigerator and should be transplanted to pots as soon as they do.

Some popular herbs just can't be grown from seed. French tarragon is virtually sterile; it seldom even flowers. Peppermint and Italian oregano (also called hardy marjoram) are hybrids and 99 percent sterile, according to Arthur O. Tucker, an herb taxonomist. In a landmark study of thyme plants, Harriet Flannery Phillips discovered that all English thyme plants have only female flowers, making it impossible to reproduce truly from seed; this condition may also account for the variability of other seed-grown thyme.

For all their complexities, seeds remain a prime means of starting herb plants because they can be stored for many months and even years. They are small and easy to ship, inexpensive, and require little special equipment to germinate and grow into plants.

SOWING SEED OUTDOORS

Because most gardeners want only a few of each kind of plant, herbs are not row crops in most gardens as are corn, beans, broccoli, lettuce, and other vegetables. If you want only two or three plants of a variety, whether annual, biennial, or perennial, it's not efficient to sow seed directly in an outside garden bed. If you want a dozen or more plants, though, direct sowing becomes more practical. The following popular annuals or biennials come easily from direct-sown seed: basil, borage, caraway, chamomile, chervil, coriander, dill, and parsley.

Many perennial herbs that come true from seed are not usually direct-sown because their seeds might be tiny and difficult to handle, and the seedlings slow to grow after they've emerged. Perennial herbs with larger seeds or more rapid growth for direct seeding are angelica, anise hyssop, chives, lemon balm, lovage, sage, and sorrel.

Preparing the Seedbed

Soil preparation is important to successful germination and growth of herb seeds. A good seedbed is level and rich in nutrients, deeply dug, quick draining, and composed of the finest earth without clods or stones. Unless you garden somewhere near the center of the universe (which is between Grundy Center and Eldora in Iowa), where Nature made the soil

A rich tapestry of herbs can result from a handful of seeds scattered on well-prepared ground.

Photography by Betsy Strauch

nearly perfect for growing anything, seedbed preparation may take some backbreaking work. Gardeners unlucky enough to live in areas of the United States that have sticky, heavy clay soil that dries brick-hard, or a sandy soil that refuses to hold moisture, need to give their ground special attention — more than just turning the soil with a fork and raking away the stones. Beds where seed will be sown need even better soil tilth than ordinary garden beds, but it is possible to create it even if your garden is located on an old, abandoned driveway, as is mine.

Unless your garden will be built on a concrete pad, it's probably not necessary to buy topsoil; I don't trust the stuff I've found in plastic bags with a topsoil label because the contents often doesn't look much different from the good old gold-colored Virginia clay with

---

Among those seeds needing light to germinate are angelica, borage, dill, echinacea, feverfew, and wormwood.

---

which I'm blessed. Instead, I put great faith in soil amendments; my favorites are good, crumbly composted vegetative matter — rotted leaves, grass clippings that have not been treated with herbicides, and vegetable kitchen scraps — and sphagnum peat that comes in compressed bales, usually from Canada.

After I've turned the top 1 foot of soil and removed stones, broken bottles, and other artifacts and reduced all the clods to grainy smoothness with a garden fork, I thoroughly work into the soil about 6 inches of damp compost or peat moss. The result is soft, smooth,

and porous. When I use this much peat moss (or composted hardwood leaves), I dust garden lime over the entire bed until it looks as if there had been a light snow. The lime will counteract the acidity of the peat or the leaves and my naturally acidic soil, resulting in a soil pH of about 6 to 6.5 — perfect for most herbs. To verify that your soil is properly balanced and neither too acid (low pH) or too sweet (high pH), call your local U.S. Agriculture Extension Service office for information on how to have your soil tested.

If you're a fan of manure and live where it is readily available, help yourself to some of the dried, composted stuff and spread a couple of inches of it over the new garden bed. Then thoroughly mix it into the top foot of soil; manure is low in nutrients and gives them up slowly, but it is a fine soil conditioner.

Finally, add an all-purpose fertilizer, either organic or inorganic; a slow-release fertilizer such as Osmocote 14-14-14 lasts through a normal gardening season. Fertilizers formulated for the soilless growing media used for container plantings often contain trace elements as well, minute quantities of minerals that plants need and usually find in normal soils.

If you can straighten up after all this digging and soil preparation, stand back and admire your newly raised garden bed. It's wise to put stones or wood around the edges to keep the new garden soil from washing away during hard rains.

Sowing seed is as low-tech as it was 2,000 years ago. All you need is a stick or a finger to scratch a row and some labels to mark the rows and identify the seedlings when they germinate. Most herb seed germinates quite well when scattered in rows and covered with ¼ inch of soil; spacing is not critical at this point, although seeds needn't be too close together.

These fine bedfellows share environmental preferences. A profusion of scented-geranium blossoms (*Pelargonium* spp.) softens the gnarly cacti.

Photography by Joseph Strauch, Jr.

For best results from a new herb garden, make a plan and prepare the soil well. See photo on the next page.

The seed of some herbs needs light to germinate, but this fact is easily misconstrued; it doesn't mean seeds need a tan before they will germinate. The large seed of borage will get enough light if planted ½-inch deep in loose soil, according to Lyle Craker of the University of Massachusetts, one of the top soil scientists in the United States. Smaller seeds should be closer to the surface. Other seeds needing light include angelica, dill, echinacea, feverfew, and wormwood.

Covering the seed with dampened soil is important, however, because it brings the seed into contact with the moisture that wakes it up to grow. Seed covered too deeply, however, may lack enough energy to send its sprout all the way up into the sunshine. The rule of thumb for most seeds is to sow them to a depth twice the seed's diameter. Seedbed soil should remain damp but not soggy until seedlings emerge. For seedlings that take several weeks, such as parsley, gardeners sometimes place a board or other cover over the row to lessen water evaporation and keep weeds down until seeds germinate. Competition for food and light from weeds is often a big problem for seedlings struggling into the world, and the prudent gardener will keep a weed-free seedbed.

After seedlings emerge, don't let them wilt from lack of water, but also do not water them too often, for root rot and fungus diseases get a quick start when soil is kept too wet. Plant roots need air; too much water fills the air pockets in the soil and can suffocate roots. It's best to water in the morning so that seedlings don't spend the night drowning; during the day, water evaporates from the soil quickly. Apply an all-purpose water-soluble fertilizer every two weeks for six weeks after germination to speed early growth.

TRANSPLANTING OUTDOOR-GROWN SEEDLINGS

If you plan to grow seedlings to maturity where you sowed them in an outdoor garden, thin them to the spacing suggested in the chart on pages 62 to 71. Thinning will permit the plants to grow without close competition for air, light, water, and nutrients. I never bother to thin dill and coriander seedlings because the plants mature so quickly, and I am interested in the early foliage growth rather than the mature growth which produces seeds. I just snip off enough foliage to use in the kitchen. The foliage will regrow on these seedlings and as many as five crops can be harvested.

Sowing seed where plants will grow eliminates the transplant step that slows growth and increases risks. But sometimes transplanting is necessary, especially if you have established a nursery area, cold frame, or special seedbed in your garden. Cloudy, damp spring days are made for transplanting seedlings from the seedbed to the main garden. Dig the seedlings with as little damage as possible to the roots; I transplant outdoor-grown seedlings in little groups of four or five to lessen shock caused by torn roots. This method, which I call "clump transplanting," is explained in detail on pages 25 to 29.

When I was a child, one of the jobs I enjoyed most in the garden was finding twigs to stick through 6-inch squares of paper to make little umbrellas, which I placed carefully over the seedlings my father had transplanted and watered. The twig-and-paper umbrellas lessened the shock of transplanting by tempering the sun's dehydrating effects. Now we have wonderful new materials like spun-bonded, polyester row covers that do this job and more. This translucent fabric permits light, air, and

The same herb garden only a few months later—filled with healthy, productive plants.

Photography by Joseph Strauch, Jr.

Shelves in a basement room, each equipped with a bank of lights, create space for thousands of seedlings.

water to pass through while it shields young seedlings from hot sun, cold winds, torrential rains, and an assortment of insects; it also gives some protection against squirrels and birds, which are sometimes spring predators of seedlings.

After seeds germinate, the gardener becomes aware quickly of the vulnerability of tender, young seedlings. One summer not long ago, I sowed several 3-foot rows with dill, coriander, and basil seeds, intending to use this test plot for a photo essay on the life of a seedling. Late one afternoon a few days later, I checked and saw that the seedlings had emerged. I decided to take some photos of the two rows of purple basil the following morning. Bright and early, with camera at the ready, I discovered that a troop of slugs had munched the basil into history overnight. The incident produced a shorter photo essay than I had intended, but it reminded me in no uncertain terms of the hazards of leaving unprotected young seedlings in the hands of Mother Nature. (Methods of controlling slugs are discussed on page 89.)

STARTING SEED INDOORS

I started gardening in the days before small, cheap plastic pots, and most gardens then were started by planting seeds directly in the soil. If you purchased seedlings, you got them at a nursery where a man with roughhewn hands scooped them up from a wooden flat, wrapped the tender young, green shoots in a piece of yesterday's newspaper, and handed them to you; failure often attended attempts to transplant these bare-root seedlings. Times have changed: It is easy to purchase little potted plants to place in the garden, and wonderful success almost always follows.

In addition, a range of simple and inexpensive techniques are available to home gardeners who wish to start their own seedlings indoors for transplanting to a backyard garden. Today there is no reason why a home gardener can't produce potted herbs as good as or better than those for sale at a nursery.

The advantages of growing your own seedlings are many. You'll have the variety you want when you want it, you won't have to wait on the weather to get started (as the outdoor gardener will), and an early start will produce a plant that grows larger earlier and provides a bigger harvest. You can start tiny, slow-growing perennial seeds (such as 98,200-seeds-per-ounce thyme or 165,000-seeds-per-ounce sweet marjoram), or slow-to-start parsley easily and early enough to give you a jump of several months over plants propagated outdoors.

For all the changes and new equipment, the basics of seed-starting remain unaltered from my boyhood or even the time of Pliny the Elder, who gardened in the first century A.D. That gardening is a balancing act is no more evident than when a gardener decides to start seedlings indoors for transplanting.

The key to success is creating an artificial environment that duplicates the most perfect conditions a seed might encounter outdoors. The light must be steady, and days should be long. Water should appear just when needed and in only the right amount. Temperatures should be ideal for germination and growth; a steady supply of nutrients to provide uninterrupted growth should be available. The air should move through the seedlings and caress their tender, new growth to keep them dry.

To achieve and manage such environmental control is a large responsibility, and it takes some skill, knowledge, and maybe a bit of artistry. The basics can be learned quickly, but a technique is perfected only through use,

Chicken-wire doors on the light benches keep out the author's wayward cats.

Fluorescent tubes are positioned no more than 4 inches above new seedlings.

observation, and failure. The indoor gardener needs to know much more than an outdoor counterpart who gambles that Nature will take care of almost everything.

My seed-starting experience began on a windowsill, and at first my plants were as leggy as a shoestring and as easily broken as a piece of dried capellini. I learned quickly that the wan, late winter light that reached inside lacked the predictability, intensity, and day length to keep plants stocky. I knew there must be a better way, and there was.

Little space is needed indoors to start seedlings. Fluorescent lights are the most important element in the indoor garden. Two 4-foot-long double-tube fluorescent fixtures placed side-by-side create about the right light intensity to produce sixty-four plants in

pots. (That's an area 12 inches wide by 40 inches long.) These fixtures can be hung by chains over a table so they can be raised and lowered as needed. Special plant lights are unnecessary; I have used cool-white fluorescent tubes for years with excellent results.

To keep the seedlings from growing gangly, position the tubes no more than 4 inches from the tops of the seedlings. As they grow and are transplanted from flats into pots, the lights must be adjusted. My own little growing area, located in my low-ceilinged, unheated basement, receives no natural light. To further conserve growing space, I've installed lights in a bunk-bed arrangement that has four levels; each one is 8 feet wide by 2 feet deep and about 6 feet high. In that space, I can produce enough seedlings for my herb business to fill 12,000 pots every two weeks. A timer controls the lights — sixteen hours on, eight hours off — and relieves me of the chore.

The Growing Medium

The idea of plants growing in a mix that contains no soil may seem contrary to nature, but for many years I have used soilless mixes for seed starting and for growing seedlings. I have been quite happy with these mixes because they are free of disease and weeds, store easily, hold moisture yet drain well, and give consistent results. Soilless media are made from natural substances such as sphagnum peat moss, composted peanut hulls, composted bark, perlite, and vermiculite.

I wet soilless mixes just before filling the germination containers, adding enough water to dampen the mix but keep it loose at the same time. Storing the wet mix invites disease organisms to take up residence. Almost any shallow, clean, disease-free container with drainage holes can be used to germinate seeds. In my work, I use virgin plastic flats that are 11 inches by 21 inches and are 2½ inches deep, but smaller containers such as pots work equally well for a small number of seedlings. Used pots can be sterilized with a solution of ½ cup of chlorine bleach to 1 gallon of water, with enough detergent added to scrub away accumulated dirt and mineral deposits.

Seedling containers should not be over 2½ inches deep and should not be filled all the way to the top. (Deeper plastic pots should be cut down.) If the sides of the container stand too far above the growing medium, air cannot circulate well through the seedlings, and disease may become a problem. The volume of growing medium is important because it affects the water-holding capacity of the seedling container. I've found that 1½ to 2 inches of growing medium in the container is about the right amount to allow good moisture control while giving the seedling roots ample room.

The simplest way to start seedlings is to sow a single variety of seed directly in a pot and grow it there until it's ready to go into the garden. Almost any herb can be direct-sown, but I've found that nasturtiums and chives work well with this method because they naturally grow in clumps and lack the traditional plant stem. The quality of herb seedlings is enhanced by transplanting because, as you'll see later, it allows the grower an opportunity to control seedling-stem elongation; this is a condition that leads to poor-quality, wispy plants that twine snakelike over the pot's edge.

For all the changes and new equipment,

the basics of seed starting remain

unaltered since the time of Pliny the Elder,

who gardened in the first century A. D.

Sowing Seed Indoors

I sow most herb seed in rows rather than scattering it over the surface of the growing medium. Air circulation through seedlings grown in rows is better, an important factor in eliminating disease problems. I use a small strip of metal that is V-shaped in cross-section to press furrows into the dampened growing medium and then scatter the seeds into the depressions.

It probably doesn't matter whether the seeds are covered with growing medium after they are sown. The moisture content in the

French gardeners experimented before 1892 with growing media that did not contain mineral soil and successfully grew azaleas in a combination of peat, leafmold, and pine needles. After World War II, American horticulturists, spurred by dwindling topsoil resources, developed soilless media for the plant-growing industry.

Most commercial soilless media are based on formulas developed at Cornell University in the late 1950s. They are comprised of sphagnum peat moss, composted bark or peanut hulls, perlite, and vermiculite. Because these substances contain few nutrients, plants grown in them require the frequent application of fertilizers. Earlier formulas created at the University of California also used peat moss, but the aggregate of choice was fine sand. Kenneth F. Baker, who was instrumental in developing the media, favored fine sand because he said it made his mix approach "loam in water and nutrient retention." He also advocated the use of some organic sources of nitrogen because the nutrient was released slowly over an extended period of time.

Over the years, I have found that commercial soilless media grow healthy, vigorous herbs without the problems of weeds and disease associated with soil-based mixes, but regular fertilization is important (fish emulsion works well).

Large quantities of growing media purchased at retail prices may break your budget, however. Gardeners have a reputation for self-reliance and do-it-yourself innovation; many actually shrink from the idea of buying something they can make themselves.

For a quick all-purpose soilless mix, combine equal parts of dry sphagnum peat and perlite. To each gallon of this mix, add a handful of Osmocote For Potting Mixes; the 17-6-10 slow-release formula contains the necessary trace elements that are missing from the soilless mix. Finish it off with a heaping tablespoon of ground limestone per gallon. Dampen the mix with warm water — using a hard spray that roughs the mix or kneading the mix energetically with your hands helps the peat take up the water — and it's ready to use.

Don't store dampened mix for prolonged periods. This quick recipe comes close to the popular Cornell Mix B. It drains well, a characteristic favored for herbs.

Soilless medium should be damp and scooped loosely into pots or seed flats. Packing prevents good aeration.

flats remains high enough that the seeds drink it up without being covered. If the seeds are left uncovered, you can actually watch them swell and see the first roots emerge. (The chart on pages 72 to 77 lists my preferences for covering seed; because it takes longer for germination to show when seeds are covered, the number of days to germination may vary when my suggestions for covering are not followed.)

How much seed to sow and how thickly to sow it are questions that I face annually. The amount of seed to sow depends on how many plants you want of a given variety and the germination rate of that variety. The seeding technique also plays a critical role. I have agonized over the placement of single seeds, struggling with the tiny specks to make sure they were separated in the rows by ½ inch or so. Although

this may be necessary when sowing seeds for which you paid ten or fifteen cents apiece — perhaps hybrid geranium seeds — most herb seed isn't that costly, and my transplanting technique doesn't work nearly as well when seeds are spaced so far apart. So make it easy and don't worry about spacing individual seeds; they can touch, and in some cases it's best to sow them so thickly that they are piled atop each other, as with parsley and other herbs that have low germination rates.

Many experienced gardeners would shudder at how thickly I sow seeds, knowing that thick stands of seedlings sometimes invite disease problems — especially when the seedling flats are in a greenhouse, where environmental conditions cannot be controlled as precisely as under lights. On the other hand, sowing

A strip of angled metal stock makes neat furrows for seeding.

Coriander seed is sown thickly into the furrows.

Covering the seeds loosely with growing medium is optional in most cases; I prefer to cover coriander.

Large seeds such as those of nasturtium can be handled differently than the smaller varieties.

Seeds are dibbled into individual pots, two per pot, at a depth three to four times the diameter of the seed.

Additional soilless mix is sprinkled over the seed depressions and patted lightly into place. These seeds should germinate in ten days and be ready to transplant (with two or more true leaves) in five or six more days.

thickly is quick and makes transplanting easy. Be sure to label each row of seedlings, or mark pots with a water-proof marker so you will remember what's in them.

After the seed is sown, water the pots or flats with a gentle, even spray; I use the sprayer at my kitchen sink. To keep the water from evaporating while waiting for the seed to germinate, I tape plastic wrap over the pots or flats. Pots or flats may also be slipped into clear plastic bags, and clear plastic domes are available for flats. If you are starting seed in winter or early spring, choose a room in the house that is bright and has warm, even heat between 70 and 80°F; place the flats or pots so that direct sunshine will not hit them.

I sometimes find it necessary to place a piece of cardboard over my flats; even winter sun can melt a plastic dome or cook seed to death. When I sow seeds in summer to produce fall plants, I place the flats in an air-conditioned room because daytime temperatures otherwise might prove too high for good germination. I often stack flats covered with humidity domes three or four high to conserve space; this does not affect germination.

Now the vigil begins; I check at least twice a day to watch for the first signs of seedling emergence. As soon as I notice the most minute evidence of germination — even if it's only a few scattered seedlings — I remove the plastic wrap or the humidity domes and place the containers under fluorescent lights. The lights produce enough heat to maintain 70 to 75°F daytime temperatures, but night temperatures when the lights are off may drop into

Planting seed thickly isn't wasteful; it makes for hearty, stocky clumps when the seedlings are transplanted.

the sixties. It's usually not necessary to water the seedlings when they first go under the lights because the plastic covering has maintained moisture levels during germination.

The temperature under the lights and the moisture level in the seedling container will determine how quickly a flat or pot of seedlings dries; it is often not necessary to water the seedlings until the second or third day after germination. It's easy to see when the seedlings need water because the peat moss in the soilless mix lightens in color as it becomes dry.

Moisture is the key to seedling growth, but too much water can lead to a quick death. How and when the seedlings are watered is critical to their survival. Although many growers use chemical drenches to control seedling diseases, I think diseases can be controlled as well by manipulating the seedling environment. I water my seedlings each morning soon after the lights come on and then let them dry during the day and through the night. This routine reduces problems with foliage diseases spread by water and checks root rot and other similar diseases. Under lights, there is steady warmth and light, and I can count on the growing medium to dry out predictably, which makes it easier to judge when and how much to water. Watering close to the dark period, inside or outside, soaks seedling roots at a time that it is difficult for the plant to lose the moisture, so the roots have more time in which the air pockets around them are filled with water — and this can become a problem. A fan set on low speed to push air through the seedlings will help the foliage dry after watering and prevent heat buildup from the lights. The fan also helps to dry the growing medium with air movement over its surface.

An even, gentle spray settles the growing medium and starts the germination process.

I'm so low-tech that I still use a little plastic watering can with a tapered spout that I've had for years. I direct the flow of water between the rows to keep from knocking down the seedlings; by adjusting the angle of the watering can, I can easily control the flow of water to prevent growing medium from washing over them. If the surface of the growing medium does not look dry the next morning, I know that I am applying too much water, so I cut back that morning, or don't water at all. Seedlings can withstand more dryness than many gardeners believe.

When you water, make sure all the growing medium is wet; water running out the bottom of a pot or flat is one indication. However, growing medium with a high peat content is sometimes difficult to wet if it has become too dry, and water applied from the top can run through without penetrating to the roots. You may need to water a second or third time to thoroughly wet the medium, particularly when the growing medium has pulled away from the pot walls as it has dried, allowing the water to run down the sides and out the bottom. Keen observation is important during watering because you've got to get it right. Overwatering is the leading cause of plant and seedling mortality.

Feeding Seedlings

A liquid fertilizer applied during watering will produce amazing results in seedling quality that will follow through into the garden. Most commercial growing media have enough fertilizer to feed plants and seedlings for a week

Plastic wrap or clear plastic lids hold moisture until seeds begin to germinate.

or two; I begin my regular feeding schedule after the seedlings have been under lights for a week. I recommend use of an organic or inorganic water-soluble fertilizer, at the manufacturer's recommended strength, applied at least once a week when you water. (Fish emulsion or Peters 20-10-20 work well, but any plant food can be used.)

The importance of feeding even little seedlings was underscored by research conducted in Israel by Eli Putievsky. His studies found that fertilizing herbs such as marjoram, lemon balm, and thyme at each watering with a nutrient solution half the recommended strength resulted in plants that were double and triple the size of unfertilized ones after sixty days. That's a tremendous head start for plants as they go into the garden.

Transplanting Indoor-Grown Seedlings

The first leaves that appear on a seedling differ in shape from the plant's later leaves and are called the cotyledons, seed leaves, or nurse leaves. The next leaves that emerge are the true leaves, and as soon as seedlings produce a set of these true leaves, it is time to transplant them. If not transplanted promptly, the seedlings will become stringy and too crowded for proper growth — and impossible to untangle for transplanting.

When transplanting seedlings into pots from their germination flats, be very careful of their roots. Because new seedlings' root systems are minimal, very little growing medium will cling to them when you move the plants. Transplanting bare-rooted seedlings can cause

A pale, dry surface signals that it's time to water; a carefully directed fine stream won't knock down tiny seedlings.

To begin clump transplanting, gently break out a row of thickly planted seedlings.

Break the row into smaller clumps, keeping as much growing medium around the roots as possible.

Gently massage the root clumps so they can be broken easily into small groups of three to five or six plants.

It's important to work quickly so that delicate roots won't dry out.

Holding a clump by its leaves, dibble a hole in each pot with an index finger or other blunt instrument.

Be sure not to pack the growing medium as you set the clumps in place.

considerable stress to young plants and must be done with care.

This problem aside, I have yet to find a seedling grown under lights indoors that can't be transplanted; this includes parsley, coriander, dill, and all the other herbs about which warnings are traditionally offered. The gardener's control of the environment indoors or in a greenhouse is the reason that it is so easy to transplant these herbs successfully.

I use plastic pots that are 2 to 2½ inches square at the top and fill them with the same soilless growing medium I used to start the

---

I settle the clump into the hole gently, but deeper than it was growing in the seedling flat. The depth to which the clump is set depends on where the nurse leaves, not the true leaves, are located on the stem.

---

seedlings, dampening it before use in the same way. Pots should be sterile to avoid disease problems; plastic pots are easier to sterilize with chlorine bleach and soap (as described on page 41) than those made from clay or foam.

My special technique for transplanting seedlings into pots, which I call "clump transplanting," lessens stress on the seedlings and creates healthier plants more quickly than traditional procedures. Plants grown this way are more likely to have larger harvests, as well. Instead of removing single seedlings and dibbling them into pots, I gently break a row of seedlings into small clumps of up to five seedlings. I don't count them but take what

comes apart most easily with the least root damage. It would defeat the beneficial effects of this method to prick out individual seedlings and gather them in clumps. The size of the clump usually depends on the physical stature of the seedlings; the larger the leaves, the fewer seedlings in the clump.

I aim to create the immediate appearance of a branched plant without having to wait many weeks for it to happen naturally through numerous prunings of the tiny stems. The clump begins with a larger root mass in the pot than a single seedling would have, so water is taken up faster. In a small way, this accelerates the drying of the growing medium and lessens the problems of root and stem rot.

The actual transplanting differs a bit from traditional methods. I hold the clump of seedlings by their leaves so as not to damage the soft stems; damaged stems offer an entry to disease organisms that cause stem rot. While I hold the clump in one hand, I shove the index finger of my free hand into the center of the pot into which the clump will go. I settle the clump into the hole gently, but deeper than it was growing in the seedling flat.

The depth to which the clump is set depends on where the nurse leaves, not the true leaves, are located on the stem. I try to place the clump deep enough that the true leaves are level with the growing medium and the nurse leaves are covered. This depth isn't always possible, but the seedlings should stand upright in the center of the pot, even after watering. I water the seedling clumps lightly immediately after transplanting to settle the growing medium around the roots.

After transplanting, I put the pots back under fluorescent lights, raising the lights if necessary to accommodate the height of the pot but still keeping the lights only a few inches from the top of the plant. I continue to water and fertilize the potted seedlings as they begin to fill out; the transplants should be ready for the garden in three to six weeks. I judge a seedling ready for the garden when its foliage has spread to the edge of the pot and when there is sufficient root growth to hold the growing medium together when the plant is gently knocked out of the pot for inspection.

Hardening Off

The one drawback to growing plants indoors under lights is that stems and leaves are soft and the plants cannot be placed in the garden as soon as they are ready; it is necessary to acclimate them to the vicissitudes of the outdoor environment. Gardeners call this process "hardening off," a term that describes the stiffening of the tender tissues of the stem and leaves.

Cold frames, basically bottomless boxes with clear lids that can be raised for ventilation, are the traditional way to protect plants while introducing them to the real world of wide temperature swings, strong sunlight, and stiff breezes. If you don't have a cold frame, you can put young potted plants in a place that receives morning sun only and is protected from wind, bringing the plants in each night; follow this procedure for three days. For the next three days, give the potted plants a more open location and leave them out at night as long as it is above freezing. This will prepare them for planting on the seventh day.

A less complicated way to harden off transplants is to place the pots in the garden and cover them with a thin layer of spun-bonded row cover. (If the weather changes to brutal cold, it's easier to bring the seedlings in if they're in pots.) Row cover not only protects tender foliage from burning but allows water to trickle through it, and at night provides some protection from cold. After four or five days under a row cover, the potted plants are ready to be transplanted. For the appropriate times to transplant specific herbs, see the chart on pages 78 to 83.

Now that your herbs are at home in the garden, you can sit back and enjoy them with the knowledge that you have worked with nature to nurture a small speck of life into something much larger and more wonderful. At the same time, you have the opportunity to watch a little part of the world with which you have an intimate relationship live in its time. You've earned that sense of pride that comes with self-sufficiency.

This coriander seedling was transplanted from flat to pot two weeks ago and is ready for the garden.

Photography by Dency Kane

Although lavender and yarrow contrast dramatically in the garden, both plants can be propagated without seed.

PLANTS FROM
PLANTS

The reproductive power of seeds is complex and mysterious, but when a bit of branch from an herb sprouts roots and becomes a plant on its own, we call it a rooted cutting and think it happens almost like magic. Herbs, and many other plants, are capable of even more asexual sorcery. To make new plants, roots (and rhizomes) can be divided, plant crowns can be separated into new plants, and branches that touch the ground can form roots and the rooted portion can become independent from the parent plant.

There is really no magic that animates the asexual reproduction of plants; it's all a matter of genes. All the genetic information about a plant is contained in each of its cells, and under the right conditions, it's possible for a segment of a plant to reproduce its missing parts and make a new plant that is genetically identical to its parent. It would be magical indeed if plants could do this whenever they wished, but they can't; certain environmental factors, including human intervention, must be present for it to happen.

Vegetative propagation is the only way in which many important culinary, medicinal, and fragrant herbs can be propagated. Perennial herbs such as artemisia, thyme, santolina, rosemary, mint, lavender, sage, and oregano have many cultivated varieties that are not reliably true to type when grown from seed; as a general rule, it's prudent to propagate all named cultivars vegetatively. Other herbs produced vegetatively are those that are sterile or those for which seed is not readily available. You'll find vegetative propagation convenient and fast if you want a few new plants from a friend's garden or a space-saving way to overwinter tender herbs indoors, or if it's time to replace a favorite sage, savory, or lavender that is becoming woody and unproductive.

Herbs with variegated foliage generally can't be propagated by seed. Cuttings or divisions are the best guarantee that the offspring will resemble the parent, as in this *Lavandula dentata* 'Linda Ligon.'

This thyme grew from a natural layering when a branch from the parent plant came in contact with the soil and rooted.

To move it to a new location, lift the plant gently to keep as much soil as possible around its roots.

Sharp shears divide one layered plant into several, each with a healthy root system.

LAYERING STEMS

Creating new plants by layering stems is ridiculously simple. Many perennial herbs, including chamomile, santolina, southernwood, winter savory, creeping and English thymes, prostrate rosemary, lavender, and Vietnamese coriander, do it without prompting. A stem touches the moist ground, and before you know it that stem has put down roots. When plants perform this multiplying feat without your assistance, count your blessings, check to see that new roots are well established, and sever the connection between mother plant and offspring with a sharp knife or scissors. Then gently dig the new plant and place it in a new home.

Upright, woody-stemmed herbs with flexible branches can also be layered with your assistance. You won't need equipment to prevent wilting, as you might with rooting cuttings; after you've set some layers, you can forget about them until it's time to move the new plants or present them as potted gifts to friends.

Gardeners soon discover the axiom that it's easy for plants to do things on their own, but as soon as a gardener steps in to urge the plant to do it, difficulties begin. This is true even of something as simple as layering. To make layering work better for you, it will help to know what factors induce plant stems to root: absence of light at the point where roots are to develop, constant soil moisture, good aeration, and moderate temperatures. It's not difficult to achieve these conditions outdoors. Soil, the key ingredient, provides the darkness and holds the moisture. If it's a good, loose soil, aeration will take care of itself. For optimum temperatures, begin layering when temperatures begin to warm in late winter or spring.

Select a stem near the ground that is young and flexible. Beginning at a point 3 to 4 inches from the tip, strip about 5 inches of foliage from the stem. After removing the leaves and saving them to use in the kitchen, use a sharp knife to scrape the thin bark off 2 or 3 inches of the underside of the leafless stem; this step, called wounding, seems to accelerate rooting in some species. Dig a small hole 2 to 3 inches deep with gently sloping sides below the prepared stem, and carefully lay the stem in the hole; occasionally, it is necessary to peg it with a U-shaped wire or hairpin so it won't move. Then cover the stem with soil. If the soil in your garden is stiff or very sandy, fill the hole with a mixture of equal parts of sphagnum peat moss and perlite. Mulch the area to keep the layering site moist or water it judiciously without soaking the plant roots and foliage; overwatering may invite disease.

Layering is not a technique for the impatient. Layered stems may form roots in several weeks or months, depending on the size of the stem and the herb chosen. When a gentle tug on the stem meets with resistance, the stem is probably rooted and it's time for a careful visual inspection. If the roots are well-formed, snip the rooted stem free and lift it gently to retain as much soil as possible around its roots. Then pot the plant or set it directly into a new location in the garden (see Transplanting Rooted Cuttings, page 53).

Commercial herb growers rarely propagate herbs by layering because a single plant can produce only a few progeny at once this way, but it is an excellent technique for most home gardeners because it is easy, requires no equipment at all, and almost always works.

DIVISIONS

While many herbs creep around, sending out roots from their stems on top of the soil, others secretly spread underground from crowns, roots, offsets, and specialized stems such as stolons and rhizomes. Mint stolons are the street gangs of the garden and take new territory with eager stealth. At first glance, the

---

The crown of a sorrel plant may produce only two or three new plants, but a vigorous tarragon or mint plant may have the potential for dozens.

---

stolons look like roots themselves, but careful inspection reveals hairy roots dangling from them. Tarragon rhizomes are fleshy, and in spring, as vernal forces wake the plant, tiny buds swell on the rhizomes and burst into new stems; these are children in need of separation from their parent. Sorrel greets the first warmth of the late winter with clusters of new sprouts from its firm ocher crown. Proper and prim, *Origanum majoricum* (often sold as hardy marjoram or Italian oregano) grows stems from a tangled mound that is easily severed into clumps that will become new plants. The many offsets of tough, slender chives are quickly divided by strong fingers into many little clumps; a single chive bulblet looks silly all alone, but will eventually multiply. Sweet woodruff, lemongrass, bee balm, 'Silver King' artemisia, and catnip are other herbs that are easy to multiply by division.

When the tiny, green-capped stems of French tarragon push their heads through the early spring soil, my heart leaps with joy; it is time to make new plants by dividing vigorous old ones. This is probably the oldest method for multiplying herbs, and certainly the easiest and quickest. Spring's cool, damp weather is the ideal time for the job, but plants can also be divided in the fall if similar climatic conditions prevail. A spade and sharp knife are the only tools you'll need for this rough surgery; the limited number of genetically identical offspring that you'll produce with them will be ready for harvesting almost immediately. Dividing herbs regularly discourages disease by thinning foliage and controlling rambunctious spreading.

The best candidates for division are herbaceous perennials, herbs, or other plants that die back each winter and pop up in the spring larger than they were the year before. Ignore thin, struggling plants with little vigor and less yen for life; instead, choose vigorous specimens with many young stems pushing their way into the spring sun.

There are two ways to go about this division business, and in all probability the method you choose gives clues to your character. If you're the kind of gardener who plans ahead (don't we all wish we did), you'll mark the plants you want to divide in the fall before their tops die back to the ground; they'll be easier to find come spring. If you're the other kind of gardener, you'll have to remember where the plants that you want to divide are located, and you'll need to be able to recognize them by their junior tufts that appear early.

If you're in a hurry, you can bluster right in and carve up a clump on the soil surface with a shovel, imagining the location of its roots from the location of its young shoots. This method may be inexact and yield few plants, but it is quick and clean. The divisions

To divide a crown of French sorrel, carefully dig up as much root as possible.

Cut into the crown vertically with a sharp knife.

Leave each part with as much root as possible.

Some Herbs That Root Easily in Water

Basil

Lavender

Lemon verbena

Mint

Pineapple sage

Rosemary

Scented geraniums

usually wind up with lots of roots for an unhindered new start.

If you've got plenty of time and want the maximum number of plants, dig gingerly around the circumference of the plant, and pry the clump carefully from the ground. Lay the mass of roots out in the shade and massage the dirt away (or wash it off with a hose). The buds that show at the top of the root clumps are guides to where to perform surgery. With a sharp knife, divide the mass of roots, stolons, or rhizomes into fragments that have several new buds each. I try to obtain as large a root system as I can with each division. The crown of a sorrel plant, for instance, may produce only two or three new plants, but a vigorous tarragon or mint plant may have the potential for dozens.

If the urge to divide your herbs strikes during hot weather, I suggest transplanting the divisions into pots and placing them in a shaded cold frame or other protected spot until the new root systems are well established. This procedure is also useful whenever your divisions have only one or two roots each. The larger the divisions, the less the transplant shock; carving up a plant with a knife or shovel can prove stressful even to a rampaging mint.

One caveat should be mentioned about divisions. Because they carry roots and garden soil with them, they can spread diseases and root insects such as nematodes from infected soils. This might be a major concern for a commercial grower with a large investment but should pose little or no anxiety for the home gardener.

ROOTING STEM CUTTINGS

I first watched a "stick" sprout roots and turn into a plant when I was a child. My mother cut the tip off an angel-wing begonia stem and put it in a glass of water on the kitchen windowsill. In a short time, it put forth a tangle of roots. Mom transplanted it to a pot, and it became a household ornament. Many years passed before I had a glimmer of the biological force that wheedles roots from a piece of stem. Now, after observing hundreds of thousands of cuttings take root, I retain a reverence and wonder for this life-creating process.

ROOTING CUTTINGS IN WATER

Mom's method of rooting begonias works quite well for many herbs, and it's virtually trouble-free. All you need are some water, a windowsill, and a small glass, jar, or styrofoam cup. I spent a recent summer experimenting with rooting herb cuttings in water, and I can tell you that this method, in some instances, will root cuttings as fast for you as my expensive, automated propagation gadgets can for me. This method almost totally eliminates plant stress, which can slow rooting, and it avoids some of the wilts and rots that plague home gardeners when they try to root cuttings in other ways.

What Works

Plant Propagation: Principles and Practices, by Hudson T. Hartmann and Dale E. Kester, a text used by students and many professional propagators, gives Mom's method a vote of confidence by stating that water is a suitable medium for rooting cuttings of easily propagated species. I've found that many herbs fit that category. Most of the herbs I tried rooted within two weeks or less: mints (a couple of varieties) in seven days; five varieties of basil in five to ten days; patchouli in ten; pineapple sage in

---

Some Herbs That Divide Easily

Bee balm

Catnip

Chives

Italian oregano

Lemon balm

Lemongrass

Mints

'Silver King' artemisia

Sorrel

Sweet woodruff

Tarragon

Basil roots well in water. Cut healthy growing tips with a sharp blade.

Strip lower leaves from the stem, leaving only the top bunch.

Place the prepared cutting into a container of clean water; a Styrofoam cup works well. Remember to change the water daily.

eleven; and lemon verbena and rosemary cultivar in fourteen days. (Although basil is usually grown from seed, some new cultivars, such as 'Silver Fox,' 'Aussie Sweetie,' 'Mulberry Dance,' and 'Holly's Painted,' to name a few, either don't flower well or don't come true from seed, so rooting their cuttings is the most reliable way to propagate them.)

Some herbs were slower or less successful. Scented geraniums took twenty-six days to root vigorously; an Italian oregano took about as long, but the roots were weak and sparse. Fruit sage took nearly four weeks. Two lavender varieties rooted in a little over six weeks, but only a small percentage of another struck roots, and weak ones at that.

A few of the herbs didn't respond at all. French tarragon, thyme, balm of Gilead, and myrtle either rotted or had failed to root after two months. Two cultivars of common sage did not root at all. Fortunately, these herbs can be propagated by division or are fairly easy to root in a peat-based medium that is misted frequently. I found that not all varieties of the same herb species rooted with the same speed or vigor, but this is also true with other propagation methods.

Some techniques that improve the rooting of cuttings in other media don't work when used with water. Scented geraniums, for instance, often root better when they are cut in the evening and allowed to sit in a plastic bag overnight to allow the wound to heal before they are stuck in a soilless medium. The cuttings that I treated this way did not root at all in water, while untreated ones did well. I knew that wounding cuttings of sweet bay by scraping either side of the stem helps them strike roots in a peat-perlite medium, but this didn't seem to make any difference in water.

The response of bay cuttings surprised me. Even under the most favorable conditions — with root-zone heating and intermittent misting — only 50 to 70 percent of my woody bay cuttings rooted in a soilless growing medium after six to eight weeks. I tried them in water, and they just sulked in their styrofoam cups without striking a single root. At the end of two months, the stems didn't appear callused, swollen, or ready to sprout roots, but the part of each stem that was under water was covered with wart-like nodes. I nearly gave up on them, but instead moved them to 2½-inch pots containing my usual growing medium. Within a month, all were nicely rooted and growing well with no special care. A 100-percent success rate with bay cuttings was a first for me.

The Procedure

Although it's quite possible to throw a cutting in a glass of water and watch it root, you're likely to have greater success with a wider range of cuttings if you pay attention to a few details. Take cuttings from plants that are in vigorous growth outdoors. Indoor plants with soft, thin stems are unsuitable for rooting; outdoor plants that are dormant or entering dormancy are often difficult or impossible to root. Generally, the best time for rooting cuttings is in spring, but I have had success with cuttings taken all through the growing season. Nonflowering stems are the best choice; remove any flower buds from other stems.

Choose plants that are free of disease and insects. As a hedge against failure, I like to cut several stems of each plant and put them all in one container unless they seem overcrowded. Cut each stem about 3 to 4 inches from the tip with a sharp pair of scissors or knife and remove the lower leaves from the part that will

Several cuttings may share the same water container. Check regularly for root development.

This close-up shows the root development of a plant that is ready to be placed into soil.

Gently tuck the rooted cutting into the soilless mix that fills its new pot.

be submerged. Then fill a glass, short jar, styrofoam cup, or other container so that the bare stem is in water but the leaves stay dry; at least the top third of the cutting should extend above the container rim. I write the name of the variety and the date on each cup with a waterproof marker. Place the containers where they will receive plenty of bright light but no direct sun. I root my cuttings on the kitchen windowsill with a northern exposure.

Changing the water every day is the key to success with rooting in water. It keeps the water free from bacteria that can cause stems to rot.

As soon as the cuttings have roots ¼ to ½ inch long, they are ready to transplant into pots; don't let them grow into a dense tangle. Cuttings rooted in water are transplanted the same way as seedlings, except that a single stem is planted in each pot. The growing tip of the rooted cutting is cut right after transplanting to encourage branching. (See page 55 to 58 for transplanting tips.)

I have often read that cuttings rooted in water do not transplant or grow well, but I have never had any problems as long as I first transplant them into a pot so that they can become established plants. I also follow this system with cuttings rooted in a soilless mix.

Place the potted cuttings in a sunny window, a few inches below fluorescent lights, or in a greenhouse. The heat in my greenhouse (often over 100°F during the day) made my summer cuttings grow quickly.

Rooting cuttings in water is a handy propagation technique for use throughout the growing season, but it is especially useful in late summer when it's time to start new plants to grow indoors over winter. With luck and a little attention, you'll have windowsills filled with rooted cuttings to enjoy during the cold months or to set out next spring, as well as some to share with friends.

ROOTING CUTTINGS IN A GROWING MEDIUM

My father-in-law, W. K. Doyle, delighted me one day with a story of how boxwood cuttings were rooted in the Shenandoah Valley of Virginia in the early part of this century. Nurserymen went door to door during the summer, asking permission to trim and shape the many boxwoods that adorned the door yards of farms and houses in small towns. They performed the task free or for a low price, and took away burlap bags filled with the clippings. They carried these to a nearby stream and stuck them in sandbars kept moist by the clear mountain water. Nature took its course, and in time the boxwoods rooted.

Today, high-tech equipment is available to accomplish the same task. One expensive machine on the market a few years ago made propagation as simple as plugging the gadget into an electric outlet and slipping a cutting in each slot; in a week or two, the cuttings rooted. Both old and modern methods used to root cuttings have this in common: They create an environment that induces roots to form.

Time, moisture, light, and temperature play important and well-known roles in encouraging cuttings to root. Other factors, such as oxygen, are less obvious to many gardeners. When there is plenty of oxygen, new roots are slender, branched, flexible, and easily transplanted, but with limited oxygen there are fewer roots and those tend to be brittle and unbranched. The amount of oxygen available to cuttings is related to the rooting medium that is used.

A rooting medium should be free of diseases and weeds, hold water but drain well, and support cuttings upright. It also should be loose enough to be well aerated, and allow cuttings to be inserted easily without bending or injuring tender stems. A pH of around 6.5 will usually produce the most roots; one that is too acidic will slow or prevent root emergence.

Indoor plants with soft, thin stems are unsuitable for rooting, and outdoor plants that are dormant or entering dormancy are often difficult or impossible to root.

A great variety of materials including sphagnum peat, perlite, vermiculite, sand, rockwool, and floral foam can be used to root cuttings. Though much used in the past, sand is rarely used today because it holds less moisture and air than do other popular media.

I favor a mixture of one part perlite and one part Pro-Mix BX, a commercial soilless growing medium that contains sphagnum peat moss, perlite, and vermiculite. I have used this mix successfully for years, but many commercial growers prefer other materials; some change their medium with the season or with the particular herb to be rooted. Perlite by itself may be a good choice in many climates during the low light and cool temperatures of winter because it provides good aeration and holds little water, which protects stems against rot, but its inability to hold water limits its use at other times of the year.

Cuttings root best when they have some leaves attached, because the leaves produce chemicals that promote root initiation and growth. Too many leaves, or very large leaves, on the other hand, speed water loss that can lead to wilting and quick death. Protecting the cutting from water loss and wilting by raising the humidity around the cuttings is most commonly achieved by misting the leaves, which also cools the leaf surfaces. Mist may be applied automatically or manually with a spray bottle each time you walk by your cuttings. Automatic mist systems that spray a fog of microscopic water particles are used in many commercial greenhouses.

Ambient air temperatures in the sixties and root-zone temperatures at 75 to 80°F are ideal for making cuttings root. For bottom heat, I use rubber heat mats plugged into a thermostat that is connected to a bulb thermometer stuck carefully into a flat of cuttings. For sunny summer days when the air temperature soars in my greenhouse, I drape a winter-white polyethylene material with 70-percent opacity high over and around my propagation bench; it reduces temperatures around the cuttings and provides enough light for rooting.

Learning to grow herbs well on a commercial scale has been a long and sometimes painful process. In the early years, I showed a visiting grower my propagation area, a shelf under a bench in the greenhouse. I still remember her perplexed response: How can you root this stuff without light? I was able to root cuttings in the semi-dark under the bench (even an occasional bay cutting), but an awful lot of cuttings died. I purchased a cheap mist system, which improved my success, but I "saw the light" only when I realized that the short daylight hours of winter and early spring were hindering rooting. Installing overhead lights to

SIMPLE ROOTING ENVIRONMENTS

Here are some inexpensive ways to emulate professional rooting methods on a small scale.

- In place of a propagation greenhouse with a fog system, construct a small polyethylene tent on a table near a window where there is bright light but no direct sun. Leave an opening on one end of the tent. Place pots containing cuttings inside the tent and aim a small room humidifier at the opening. Because natural light is almost always insufficient indoors, you could include fluorescent lights as the "roof" of the poly tent.

- Make a container for rooting a few cuttings by folding an 8-by-24-inch polyethylene sheet in half lengthwise. Place a dampened mixture of equal parts of perlite and sphagnum peat in the fold. Stick prepared cuttings (see pages 44 to 46) into the rooting medium and then carefully roll up the sheet, slip a rubber band around the roll, and place it upright in a humid, cool, shaded area so the sun will not cook the cuttings.

- Place a pot of cuttings in a plastic bag. Stick two arches made from coat hanger or other flexible wire in the pot to support the top of the plastic bag so it won't touch the stem leaves. Place the pot in bright light but out of direct sun. Spritz the cuttings each day and then close the bag with a clothespin or twist tie; leave the bag open each night.

- Maintaining enough humidity around cuttings to keep them from wilting is a major problem for the home gardener. Here's a way, adapted from a number of methods, that meets the challenge. Gather the following: a 6-inch plastic pot with its drainage holes plugged (florists' clay works well), a 3-inch clay pot, and enough dampened rooting medium to half fill the large pot.

  Scoop enough medium from the center of the large pot to fill the clay pot, then insert the clay pot up to its rim in the cavity. Stick cuttings in the clay pot and place the large pot under fluorescent lights with 3 inches between them and the large pot rim. Keep the medium damp around the small pot so it will humidify the air around the cuttings.

- Several mail-order companies offer a plastic dome to hold humidity and a heat mat to maintain heat at the root zone. This combination is similar to what a professional grower might use on a larger scale.

A 3-inch stem tip of *Origanum vulgare* ssp. *hirtum* is easy to handle for rooting. Sharp scissors make a clean cut.

Strip the leaves off the lower half of the cutting by sliding thumb and index finger down the stem.

extend short winter days led to quicker and firmer rooted cuttings.

I now realize that light intensity and day length work together with root-zone heating and cool air temperatures to create the perfect rooting environment. The twelve- to fourteen-hour day is ideal for rooting cuttings, and as long as air temperatures are cool, the cuttings under mist stand tall. As air temperatures warm, I cut light levels (not day lengths) with shade cloth or white plastic to keep cuttings turgid.

Good gardeners recognize that it is important to supply nutrients to their plants, but this is not usually considered in the propagation of herb cuttings. Eli Putievsky, the Israeli researcher, discovered that small amounts of fertilizer applied every two days to sage cuttings increased the number of cuttings that rooted from 79 percent to 90 percent. Of those that rooted, the fertilized cuttings averaged 128 percent more roots than the unfertilized ones. Fertilizing cuttings is worth trying with other herbs, too, but be careful not to soak the rooting medium. Root-zone heating, which helps to dry the rooting medium, is a must with this technique.

Selecting and Preparing Cuttings

It takes a healthy stem cutting to produce a high-quality plant. The best plants from which to take cuttings have been getting plenty of sun and are plump with vigorous new, compact growth. Avoid plants that are wilted or appear

Dipping the stem in rooting hormone is beneficial to the rooting process or the gardener's peace of mind, or both.

The cutting is stuck deeply into a pot or flat of loose soilless medium so that the leaves almost touch the surface of the medium.

stressed in any way, have yellow or moldy brown leaves, or have spindly or weak branches. Stems that make the best cuttings are supple and strong but not woody. New growth — often referred to as soft-wood or herbaceous — is generally best for cuttings because it is most likely to root quickly and be free of pests. How to select the best stems to cut is hard to teach, because it is a visual and tactile skill amplified by intuition and experience.

Many books suggest using razor-sharp knives to take cuttings. Perhaps I break too many rules, but I have always used scissors for this purpose, except when cutting the thick, woody stems of bay, and it hasn't hurt my rooting averages. Most herb stems are tender and succulent rather than thick and tough, so sharp

scissors cut cleanly and make a nice wound, which encourages the cells to multiply and make roots.

Selecting the best stems to cut takes some time, but it's important to work quickly so that the cuttings don't wilt before they can be stuck and put in an atmosphere of high humidity. I usually work in the early morning, but early evening might be even better with twelve hours of darkness to help the cuttings adjust to their new status.

I try to cut stems to a uniform length, somewhere between 3 and 4 inches, but this varies with the herb variety and the condition of the stems on the mother plant. I pay little attention where I cut on the stem; above a node or leaf or below it doesn't seem to matter when it comes to making roots. The woodier and tougher part of the stem below this tip is slower to root, and the longer a cutting takes to root, the more danger it faces from disease. Disinfecting the cutting tool with alcohol after each cut decreases the possibility of spreading disease from one plant to another.

The best time of year to take cuttings of most herbs is when plants are growing rapidly, daytime temperatures are still between 55 and 70°F, and nighttime temperatures are above freezing; cool weather is least stressful to cuttings. Stem tips cut during fall, when days are shorter and nighttime temperatures have dropped into the thirties, often root slowly because growth has been slowed by approaching dormancy. Where nighttime humidity is high, fall is also the time when foliage diseases are most likely to cause problems.

The traditional way of propagating lavender and many other woody shrubs is to take dormant wood cuttings in the fall and stick them in open outdoor cold frames. Over winter and spring, these would root and be transplanted into the fields. Now, with mist systems and plastic pots to speed and ease the process, I've found that spring is a better time for taking lavender cuttings. Those taken from lavender's new spring growth root quickly and easily. This is the growth that will produce flowers, of course, and I remove the flower buds before I stick the cuttings.

Cuttings are extremely vulnerable to heat and strong sunlight once severed from the mother plant, so I move to a shady spot to prepare the cuttings for insertion into the rooting medium. I strip leaves from the lower half of the cuttings by quickly sliding my thumb and index finger down the stem. It takes some practice to get the pressure just right; the goal

PROPAGATING BAYS

Propagating cuttings of sweet bay (Laurus nobilis) takes some special techniques and patience. Ordinarily, mature bays tend to grow in spurts with enough time for wood to stiffen to a snap break before a second flush of growth begins. Bays recovering from a hard winter, however, often grow continuously, and their stems do not harden sufficiently to make cuttings that will root successfully.

The most promising material for cuttings is half-hard stems that have lost the gloss of youth and tenderness and have

To propagate a sweet bay, choose half-hard stems whose leaves have lost their tender, light green look.

Remove leaves from the lower half of the stem by stripping down the stem with your thumb and finger.

Scrape two opposite sides of the bare stem with a sharp utility knife to expose the the white under-layer.

become a bit middle-aged — stiff with a dull green hue. This stage occurs about when stem buds begin to swell with new energy.

A tough bay stem is easily crushed with scissors or regular pruners, but a razor-sharp utility knife will make a beautiful, clean cut and come in handy later for preparing the cutting for rooting. Remove the leaves from the lower part of the stem as for other cuttings, and then scrape opposite sides of the lower part of the green stem with the knife to expose the white underlayer. This allows more water to be absorbed by the cutting and also encourages the interior cells of the stem to begin division and root production.

For many years, I used the strongest rooting hormone I could find to help tough-to-root bays, but when a grower acquaintance questioned this, I tested my assumption. I found that indole-3-butyric acid, the active hormone in my rooting powder, actually hindered bay root development. The factors that promoted the quickest and best roots under mist were wounding the stem and providing root-zone heat. One-third more cuttings rooted with wounding, and root-zone heat cut rooting time by one-third. I've found that bay cuttings do well under mist, but they will also root if left in a cool, damp spot that is protected from drying breezes and direct sun.

This oregano cutting has struck roots after a week to ten days but is not yet ready to transplant. Note that the rooting medium still clings to the stem.

Pruning an oregano as soon as it's transplanted to its growing pot will help it branch and get bushy.

Knock rooted cuttings from their pots to see if they're ready to transplant to the garden. Enough roots should show around the edges to hold the growing medium together.

is to remove the leaves without damaging the stems, creating a cutting that has a bare stem on the cut end and nice green leaves hugging the stem from the midpoint up to the growing tip. If I'm going to root these cuttings in water, I do it forthwith.

If I plan to place the cuttings in rooting medium, I dip the bare part of the stem in rooting powder that contains less than 1 percent indole-3-butyric acid, a naturally occurring plant rooting hormone. This makes me feel good, but I don't know that it actually helps herbs to root. Most herbs root easily, and I've not systematically evaluated the benefits of using rooting powder except on rosemary and bay cuttings. I've found that the roots on untreated rosemary cuttings tend to be less bushy than the roots from treated cuttings, but bay cuttings treated with hormones are less likely to root than untreated ones. Researchers can provide impressive photos to show the efficacy of applying rooting hormones, so I'll keep dipping my cuttings — just in case.

I've watched demonstrations of sticking cuttings and talked to growers about it, and I've come to the conclusion that with time you develop your own style of doing it. Many propagators use a dibble — a pointed stick about the size of a pencil — to punch a small hole in the soil or rooting medium so the rooting powder won't rub off when the cutting is stuck. I don't worry about this because even if the rooting hormone does rub off, it remains in the rooting area. But dibbles are useful for seating thin or weak stems of herbs like thyme and oregano; when stuck into a dibbled hole, the stem won't bend or break, either of which would put an end to any chance of rooting.

I usually stick my herb cuttings in open plastic flats that measure 11 inches by 21 inches by 2½ inches deep; from 100 to 300 cuttings will fit in such a container, depending on the size of the cutting and the herb variety. Any sterile container that is no deeper than 2 or 3 inches may be used to root cuttings: pots, cell packs, or plug trays with tiny cells made to hold a single cutting each. I try to make the best use of my valuable greenhouse space, so I tend to keep cuttings close together. Pots take up the most space.

I space cuttings far enough apart that their leaves don't quite touch; this permits some air to circulate through them, which lessens the likelihood of disease in the super-humid propagation atmosphere. Pots that are at least

---

I pay little attention where I cut on the stem — above a node or leaf or below — it doesn't seem to matter when it comes to making roots.

---

2 inches deep are useful for rooting just a few cuttings; those deeper than 3 inches may keep the rooting medium too wet and prevent proper aeration.

After the cuttings are all stuck in the flat, plug tray, or pot, I water them with a gentle flow from a hose fitted with a water breaker. The water gently settles the rooting medium around the base of the cuttings without packing it. After the cuttings are firmed by the water, they go into the high-humidity environment described on page 43.

Tending the Cuttings

In the cool, humid propagation area and the darkness of the rooting medium, some cut

Cuttings can be stuck two or three to a pot with their leaves just touching but with plenty of room for air circulation.

VARIETAL SELECTION

Besides choosing stems that are vigorous and healthy, varietal appearance is also important, especially in variegated herbs, many of which have occasional stems that are atypical. Golden lemon thyme, for instance, often has poor variegation on some stems and may even have stems with solid green leaves; these atypical stems will remain green if you root them. On the other hand, an extraordinarily beautiful or unusually variegated stem can be propagated by rooting. In fact, this is how many new cultivars are made available to the public.

Years ago I ordered some cuttings of 'Rober's Lemon Rose' scented geranium. In the first shipment, I received rooted cuttings that were typical, but the next shipment of cuttings resembled another scented geranium, 'Old Fashioned Rose.' I asked the propagator to explain the mixup and was told that he had two "forms" of 'Rober's Lemon Rose,' one with a "cut leaf" and one with a "potato leaf." What he had, of course, were two separate scented geranium varieties, even though both had come from the same parent. Just because a plant has a name doesn't mean that a stem which shows a genetic change should carry the same name. Such a variance could qualify as a new variety, or it could simply resemble its pre-hybridization parent.

tings will inevitably die. On my daily check of my greenhouse propagation area, I remove any cuttings that are dead, because these will become vectors for disease that can spread rapidly to the other cuttings in the dampness. I check the rooting medium to make sure it is still moist. If it has begun to dry out, I water and fertilize at the same time.

My ideal is that the mist will barely have dried on the leaf surfaces of my cuttings before the next burst of moisture falls — a difficult condition to maintain when you're misting by hand. Some propagators feel that it is beneficial to allow the cuttings to wilt moderately between waterings, believing that this stress stimulates rooting and makes a tougher plant. I belong to the school that believes in pampering cuttings, not stressing them. I do everything I can to prevent the cuttings from wilting,

'Golden Rain' rosemary (*Rosmarinus officinalis* 'Joyce DeBaggio')

Sometimes genetic changes, when they represent a new variety, are worth propagating. For instance, I found a single stem on an otherwise entirely dark-green rosemary plant that sported golden margins and green centers. That stem became my 'Golden Rain' rosemary (*Rosmarinus officinalis* 'Joyce DeBaggio'). Had I been unable to root this single stem tip, this highly decorative and aromatic evergreen shrub would not have come to be. Hybridizing seeds may be the classic method for obtaining new varieties, but genetic variations, or sports, are sometimes just as important. And any gardener may be lucky enough to discover sports like this one.

Herbs grow best when they go from a small-sized to an intermediate pot. To begin, gently tip or knock the well-rooted little plant from its pot.

Place the plant gently into the larger pot.

Settle the plant in and trim the top shoots to encourage bushy growth.

including misting frequently and hanging shade cloth or white poly over the propagation area during hot weather.

After the first week, I get anxious and begin to check the progress of my cuttings; I tug a few at random to see if there is any resistance caused by new roots. I remove a cutting or two, looking for a callus, an ugly mass of cells that swells the stem and eventually cracks with roots. I'm elated when I find cuttings with roots; I know that I've been successful at working with nature again. Soon I'll see top growth — although sometimes it starts even before roots form.

When the roots are from $\frac{1}{4}$ to $\frac{1}{2}$ inch long, the cuttings are ready to transplant, and I remove them from their pampered rooting environment. A delay of a day or two in moving cuttings from the humid propagation area can sometimes be all that is needed for disease to sweep through. Sometimes I leave the flats on heat mats to encourage roots to continue developing rapidly, or if roots are vigorous, I put the flats on a sunny bench in the greenhouse for a few days before transplanting the cuttings to $2\frac{1}{2}$-inch pots.

Transplanting Rooted Cuttings

I transplant rooted cuttings into pots filled with my favorite peatlite mix, handling them much as I do seedlings (see pages 25 to 29), with a few exceptions. I still use my finger as a dibble, but I put a single cutting instead of a clump into each hole. I cut the growing tip at the top of each cutting to encourage it to branch at the same time that it is filling the pot with roots; with most herb varieties, this produces a nice branched plant in a few weeks. As I move the rooted cuttings from the flat to pots, I try to keep as much of the rooting medium with the roots as possible. My goal is to have an empty flat when all the cuttings are transplanted.

After a cutting has been transplanted and pruned, it is on its own to grow in the sun or under fluorescent lights. It gets fertilizer once a week and water as needed. To see whether a new plant is ready to transplant to the garden, I knock it gently from the pot to check root development; I want to see enough roots at the edge of the root ball to hold the growing medium together. At the other end of the plant, I want to see enough foliage to cover the top of the growing medium and reach the edge of the pot. I transplant rooted cuttings

I space cuttings far enough apart that their leaves don't quite touch, permitting plenty of air circulation.

into the garden just as I do seedlings (pages 25 to 29).

Many years ago, in the quiet time before my hobby got out of hand and turned into a business, I would look at my herb garden and see delightful shapes and smell rich fragrances, and dream of ways to use them. My professional experiences in growing new plants vegetatively have changed my perspective. When I look at my herb garden today, I see the potential for making new plants from branches, crowns, and roots. The propagation game is so challenging and productive that I would encourage even the greenest herb neophyte to try making the kindest cut, the separation that creates new life.

When strong, young plants are successfully transplanted into the garden, they quickly grow to healthy maturity.

TRANSPLANTING

AND THE FIRST YEAR

When herbs are ready to transfer to the garden, outdoor temperatures should be appropriate to maintain continuous growth for the species. A setback caused by cold could seriously slow development or be fatal to sensitive plants. Some herbs, such as chervil, parsley, and sorrel, grow best in cool weather, while others, such as basil, need nearly tropical temperatures for best growth. With careful planning, you can avoid having plants ready to transplant at a time when inhospitable weather rules the garden.

Planning for transplant day begins months before you sow the first seed or take the first cutting. Getting the timing right is tough because even within a single state there can be a wide range of weather conditions. Temperatures may vary as much five to ten degrees in two places on a 50- by 100-foot lot, if my yard is any gauge. After you've gardened in the same spot for a number of years, experience and intuition will become reliable guides; until then, the accompanying charts may be helpful.

Determining when to sow seed so that transplants will be ready at the proper time (if the weather plays no tricks) is as easy as counting the days on a calendar. Find the herb you plan to propagate on the appropriate chart (page 62 to 71) and note the number of days it takes from seed to transplant. Look up the appropriate transplant temperature for that herb on the chart. For instance, lemon balm should be transplanted when nighttime temperatures are 50°F — sometime after growers in your area transplant cabbage and before they transplant tomatoes. Now mark your calendar with the transplant date and count

---

I favor soil that is well worked and so full of humus that using a trowel or a large dibble is unnecessary; just a hand will do fine, thank you.

---

backward the number of days from sow to transplant. This day is the seeding day or day to stick cuttings. Weather is always uncertain, but you'll have a couple of weeks of slack if nature tricks you. If your seedlings start to become overgrown during a wait, use scissors to snip some stems to enjoy in meals while you wait for the bad weather to break. Timing the gathering of cuttings is less certain because it's harder to control when roots will appear. Time and experience will teach you to gauge this.

INTO THE GARDEN

This isn't a book about garden planning, so I'll simply advise you to place the herbs carefully in the design that makes you happy, allowing room for air currents around them when they reach maturity. I favor soil that is well worked and so full of humus that using a trowel or a large dibble is unnecessary; just a hand will do fine, thank you. To plant, I carefully knock the plant from its pot and never pull it out by the stem, which might rip it from its roots. Then I spread the roots by tearing them a bit at the bottom of the root ball if they are circling it inside, and then place the plant in a hole so that it rests slightly lower than it was growing in the pot. I might throw a little composted manure or a few beads of slow-release fertilizer into the hole with the roots; added nutrients usually depend on the general level of soil fertility.

If the stems are long enough, I prune them after transplanting to give the plant a little shape and start the stems branching. When I water a new plant for the first time right after transplanting it, I use a liquid fertilizer instead of plain water.

THE FIRST YEAR

The first — and only — year of an annual herb has a lot crammed into it: birth, youth, old age, and death. For an annual, "life" is a four-letter word.

The first year for the typical, slower-growing perennial herb, however, is one of dependence and struggle to become established. During this year you can do much to guide the plant toward future health and vigor. The following advice is generally good for both annuals and perennials.

Well-prepared soil is so loose you can dig it with your hand. Some well-rotted manure or a few beads of slow-release fertilizer will help the plant get off to a good start.

Monitor plants regularly and make certain they do not wilt from lack of water during summer's heat. Good gardeners get that way because they have observed their plants carefully over many years. Regular examination of your plants can help you identify problems as they begin, when it is easier to combat them.

Pinch or cut stem tips regularly to encourage branching. This pruning strengthens stems and creates more foliage while building plant health and vigor. Careful pruning of woody perennials for shape during this first year can set the pattern for the plant in years to come.

Fertilize fortnightly with liquid nutrients. Contrary to some conventional advice, feed-

To transplant a hardened-off oregano to the garden, first amend and dig the soil deeply, then gently knock the plant from its pot.

Spread the roots by gently tearing and spreading the base of the root ball. Insert the plant slightly deeper than it was growing in the pot. A shallow depression encircling the plant's stem will channel moisture to the roots.

ing your herbs will not change or diminish their aroma. Though they may be able to survive between a rock and a hard place in the wild — and in your garden — they will reward generous feeding with bountiful harvests. In the second and succeeding years, perennials are often satisfied with a single application of fertilizer or organic nutrients at the beginning of the growing season, but fast-growing annuals and biennials used for their leaves, such as basil, parsley, coriander, dill, and chervil, benefit from fortnightly feedings.

Fungus diseases may attack young plants during damp, cloudy, warm weather. Diseases make themselves known when foliage begins to turn yellow and die, and when the plant wilts for no apparent reason. Herbs with dense foliage or weak stems that touch the ground are vulnerable to diseases that prey on foliage hidden from light or near the ground. Keep low-lying stems pruned and check areas of the plant that receive reduced light so that when a problem arises you find it when it is small. Then excise it. Also avoid excessive watering from above, which keeps foliage wetter than it should be. Improve air circulation around herbs by pruning to open up the interior of the plants.

Most herbs don't compete well with weeds. Traditional mulches of organic matter aren't a good guard against weeds because they tend to foster diseases on plants whose foliage rests on or near the ground. Hand weeding around

---

Hand weeding around herbs has its aromatic pleasures, and it will always be welcome and necessary.

---

herbs has its aromatic pleasures, and it will always be welcome and necessary. A 1-inch-thick mulch of sand or light-colored gravel helps smother weeds and also reflects drying heat into the interior of dense plants, controlling diseases spread by moisture.

Night-feeding slugs can be problems all season long, but they are particularly active during cool, damp weather. Spring transplants and young seedlings are vulnerable to these slimy creatures' voracious appetites. Saucers of beer, broken eggshells, midnight searches with flashlights, and diatomaceous earth are all recommended slug deterrents, but nothing works

against slugs better than thin sheets of 4-inch-wide copper. Garden centers and mail-order firms sell copper for this purpose, and copper flashing is available at roofing supply stores. Stand the copper upright and press it into the ground far enough so that it will stand up to fence in the garden bed or plants to be protected. Of course, make sure no slugs are under mulch or elsewhere inside the copper fence. As elsewhere in life and art, success often teeters on achieving a balance of opposites, and in the garden, you want the balance to tip in your favor without having to set off atom bombs.

In the first year, be patient and remember that failure is an invitation to learn more about yourself and the plants you cultivate. As Charles Dudley Warner saw it in his wise and humorous book, *My Summer in a Garden*, "The most humiliating thing to me about a garden is the lesson it teaches of the inferiority of man. Nature is prompt, decided, inexhaustible. She thrusts up her plants with a vigor and freedom that I admire; and the more worthless the plant, the more rapid and splendid its growth."

The strong roots of this divided clump of society garlic will adapt well to their new home.

EXPLAINING THE
CHARTS

A few words about the following charts may provide some interpretive assistance. There are many things a gardener wants to know about herbs other than their aroma and which variety is "best." Charts, for all their ability to convey information with precision and brevity, omit nuances on which good gardening depends. The column that lists the light requirement for acceptable growth, for instance, makes many compromises. The sun does not provide rays of light of equal intensity each hour, so it is best to use the numbers as a guide and evaluate the outcome by the growth of the herbs. If growth does not reach your expectations, you probably need a sunnier location.

Spacing herb plants is an inexact art, but it is important to their health and vigor. Plants grow differently in response to climatic conditions, but pruning can make a rambler or a sprawler dress up and conform to a more confined existence. The spacing dimensions should be taken as guides, not absolutes.

The hardiness of herbs (and other plants) is every bit as inexact as spacing, and the numbers on my chart reflect this. There are so many weather variables that killing temperatures may vary by 20 degrees or more because cold winter winds rob dormant plants of irreplaceable, life-sustaining moisture. The temperatures I've listed, however inexact they may be, are for plants in the ground, not potted ones whose roots are less protected. Predicting hardiness is often just a good guess; it's prudent to prepare for and expect the worst.

The charts show my personal preferences for covering seed for germination. Covering seeds started indoors is less critical than covering those outdoors because moisture is more easily regulated inside. On the other hand, light will penetrate the little growing medium used as a cover and reach seeds needing it.

There's no exact date on which it would be safe to transplant a particular herb into gardens nationwide. This explains why I have chosen to list nighttime air temperatures and relate planting dates to popular vegetables. Weather is fickle and it is important to be conservative when dealing with it and important plants.

GENERAL INFORMATION FOR SOME COMMON HERBS

Common name *Botanical name*	Life Span	Propagation
ANGELICA *Angelica archangelica*	*B*	*Seed*
ANISE HYSSOP Agastache foeniculum	P	Seed
BASIL *Ocimum basilicum*	*A*	*Cutting, seed*
BAY Laurus nobilis	P	Cutting, seed, division
BEEBALM *Monarda spp.*	*P*	*Cutting, division*
BORAGE Borago officinalis	A	Seed
BURNET *Poterium sanguisorba*	*P*	*Seed*
CATNIP Nepeta cataria	P	Cutting, division, seed
CHAMOMILE, GERMAN *Matricaria recutita*	*A*	*Seed*
CHAMOMILE, ROMAN Matricaria nobile	P	Division, layering, seed
CHERVIL *Anthriscus cerefolium*	*A*	*Seed*

Light Requirement	Hardy To	Mature Height	Spacing
Part sun	*-30°F*	*60"*	*36"*
Part/full sun	-20°F	36"	12"
Full sun	*35°F*	*24"*	*18"*
Part/full sun	15°F	480"	NA
Shade/part/full sun	*-20°F*	*36"*	*12"*
Full sun	30°F	24"	12"
Part/full sun	*-40°F*	*36"*	*18"*
Part/full sun	-40°F	36"	18"
Part/full sun	*32°F*	*30"*	*18"*
Part/full sun	-40°F	12"	6"
Part sun	*20°F*	*24"*	*9"*

GENERAL INFORMATION FOR SOME COMMON HERBS

Common name *Botanical name*	Life Span	Propagation
CHIVES *Allium schoenoprasum*	P	Division, seed
COMFREY *Symphytum* spp.	P	Division, seed
CORIANDER (CILANTRO) *Coriandrum sativum*	A	Seed
COSTMARY *Tanacetum balsamita*	P	Cutting, division
CURRY PLANT *Helichrysum italicum*	P	Cutting
DILL *Anethum graveolens*	A	Seed
FENNEL *Foeniculum vulgare*	P	Division, seed
FEVERFEW *Tanacetum parthenium*	P	Cutting, seed
GERANIUM, SCENTED *Pelargonium* spp.	P	Cutting, seed
HYSSOP *Hyssopus officinalis*	P	Cutting, seed
LADY'S MANTLE *Alchemilla vulgaris*	P	Division

Light Requirement	Hardy To	Mature Height	Spacing
Full sun	-40°F	18"	12"
Part/full sun	-40°F	60"	36"
Part/full sun	-40°F	36"	12"
Part/full sun	-20°F	36"	24"
Full sun	10°F	18"	12"
Full sun	29°F	36"	12"
Full sun	-10°F	48"–60"	15"
Part/full sun	0°F	36"	18"
Full sun	25°F	30"	20"
Part/full sun	-20°F	24"	24"
Part/full sun	-35°F	18"	12"

GENERAL INFORMATION FOR SOME COMMON HERBS

Common name *Botanical name*	Life Span	Propagation
LAMBS' EARS *Stachys byzantina*	P	Division, seed
LAVANDIN *Lavandula xintermedia*	P	Cutting, layering
LAVANDER, ENGLISH *Lavandula angustifolia*	P	Cutting, layering, seed
LAVENDER, FRINGED *Lavandula angustifolia*	P	Cutting, layering, seed
LAVENDER, SPANISH *Lavandula stoechas*	P	Cutting, layering
LEMON BALM *Melissa officinalis*	P	Cutting, division, seed
LEMON VERBENA *Aloysia triphylla*	P	Cutting, layering
LOVAGE *Levisticum officinale*	P	Division, seed
MARJORAM *Origanum majorana*	P	Cutting, seed
MEXICAN MINT MARIGOLD *Tagetes lucida*	P	*Cutting, layering, seed*
MINT *Mentha spp.*	P	Division, cutting

Light Requirement	Hardy To	Mature Height	Spacing
Full sun	-35°F	18"	18"
Full sun	0°F	30"–48"	24"
Full sun	0°F -30°F	30"	24"
Full sun	20°F	24"	18"
Full sun	15°F	24"–30"	18"
Shade/part/full sun	-20°F	24"	18"
Full sun	25°F	60"	36"
Part/full sun	-35°F	72"	36"
Full sun	20°F	12"	10"
Part shade/full sun	*15°F*	*18"*	*10"*
Part/full sun	-20°F	24"	15"

GENERAL INFORMATION FOR SOME COMMON HERBS

Common name *Botanical name*	Life Span	Propagation
MYRTLE *Myrtus communis*	P	Cutting, layering, seed
OREGANO *Origanum vulgare* ssp. *hirtum*	P	Cutting, division, layering, seed
PARSLEY *Petroselinum crispum*	B	Seed
ROSEMARY *Rosmarinus officinalis*	P	Cutting, layering
RUE *Ruta graveolens*	P	Cutting, layering, seed
SAGE *Salvia officinalis*	P	Cutting, layering, seed
SANTOLINA *Santolina* spp.	P	Cutting, layering, seed
SAVORY, SUMMER *Satureja hortensis*	A	Cutting, seed
SAVORY, WINTER *Satureja montana*	P	Cutting, layering, seed
SORREL *Rumex acetosa*	P	Division, seed
SOUTHERNWOOD *Artemisia abrotanum*	P	Cutting, division, layering

Light Requirement	Hardy To	Mature Height	Spacing
Part/full sun	26°F	72"	48"
Full sun	-20°F	24"	12"
Part/full sun	15°F	18"	12"
Part/full sun	10°F–15°F	48"–72"	36"
Full sun	-20°F	36"	18"
Full sun	-20°F–10°F	30"	24"
Part/full sun	-5°F	24"	18"
Full sun	33°F	18"	12"
Full sun	-10°F	18"	12"
Part/full sun	-20°F	18"	12"
Full sun	-20°F	48"	36"

GENERAL INFORMATION FOR SOME COMMON HERBS

Common name *Botanical name*	Life Span	Propagation
TANSY *Tanacetum vulgare*	P	Cutting, division, seed
TARRAGON, FRENCH *Artemisia dranunculus* var. *sativa*	P	Cutting, division
THYME, ENGLISH *Thymus* 'Broad-leaf English'	P	Cutting, layering
THYME, FRENCH *Thymus vulgaris* 'Narrow-leaf French'	P	Cutting, layering, seed
WOODRUFF *Galium odoratum*	P	Cutting, division
WORMWOOD *Artemisia absinthium*	P	Division, seed
YARROW *Achillea* spp.	P	Division, seed

Light Requirement	Hardy To	Mature Height	Spacing
Part/full sun	-20°F	48"	24"
Full sun	-20°F	24"	24"
Part/full sun	-20°F	24"	18"
Part/full sun	-20°F	16"	18"
Shade	-35°F	8"	9"
Part/full sun	-20°F	50"	36"
Part/full sun	-50°F	36"	24"

Herbs Commonly Grown from Seed

Common name Botanical name	Seeds per ounce	Viability[1]	Cover/Uncover
ANISE HYSSOP *Agastache foeniculum*	70,000	70%	Uncovered
BASIL, SWEET *Ocimum basilicum*	17,750	60%	Uncovered
BORAGE *Borago officinalis*	1,600	70%	Covered
CATNIP *Nepeta cataria*	41,000	40%	Uncovered
CHAMOMILE, GERMAN *Matricaria recutita*	275,000	40%	Uncovered
CHERVIL *Anthriscus cerefolium*	10,000	65%	Covered
CHIVES *Allium schoenoprasum*	22,000	50%	Covered
CORIANDER (CILANTRO) *Coriandrum sativum*	1,700	70%	Covered
DILL *Anethum graveolens*	21,800	60%	Covered
FENNEL *Foeniculum vulgare*	8,000	80%	Covered

Germination time at 70°F[2]	Germination to potting up	Potting up to garden[3]	Nighttime temperature at transplant[4]
6 days	20 days	14 days	55°F
4 days	18 days	14 days	65°F
5 days	15 days	11 days	55°F
5 days	25 days	14 days	50°F
4 days	20 days	14 days	45°F
7 days	10 days	12 days	45°F
6 days	Direct seeded	25 days	45°F
6 days	13 days	10 days	50°F
5 days	11 days	16 days	50°F
6 days	14 days	20 days	50°F

HERBS COMMONLY GROWN FROM SEED

Common name Botanical name	Seeds per ounce	Viability[1]	Cover/Uncover
FEVERFEW *Tanacetum* spp.	145,000	60%	Uncovered
LEMON BALM *Melissa officinalis*	50,000	60%	Uncovered
LOVAGE *Levisticum officinale*	8,000	50%	Covered
MARJORAM *Origanum majorana*	165,000	50%	Uncovered
OREGANO *Origanum vulgare*	354,000	50%	Uncovered
PARSLEY *Petroselinum crispum*	15,000	60%	Covered
SAGE *Salvia officinalis*	3,400	60%	Covered
SAVORY, SUMMER *Satureja hortensis*	47,500‘	55%	Uncovered
SAVORY, WINTER *Satureja montana*	49,700	55%	Uncovered
SORREL *Rumex acetosa*	33,000	65%	Uncovered

Germination time at 70°F[2]	Germination to potting up	Potting up to garden[3]	Nighttime temperature at transplant[4]
5 days	20 days	24 days	55°F
7 days	21 days	15 days	50°F
8 days	21 days	12 days	45°F
5 days	12 days	14 days	55°F
4 days	30 days	14 days	50°F
8 days	12 days	14 days	50°F
8 days	12 days	14 days	50°F
6 days	21 days	19 days	55°F
5 days	30 days	24 days	55°F
2 days	14 days	14 days	45°F

HERBS COMMONLY GROWN FROM SEED

Common name *Botanical name*	Seeds per ounce	Viability[1]	Cover/Uncover
THYME, FRENCH *Thymus vulgaris* 'Narrow-leaf French'	98,200	50%	Uncovered
WORMWOOD *Artemisia absinthium*	191,400	30%	Uncovered

[1] Average viability based on data from Park Seed Co., Johnny's Selected Seed, and interviews with herb growers.

[2] Production times are for optimum indoor conditions. Seedlings are clump transplanted.

[3] Plants should be hardened off for about a week before being planted in the garden (see page 53).

[4] Transplanting temperatures are estimates based on average nighttime lows and are related to transplanting common vegetables as follows: broccoli or cabbage, 45°F; tomato or pepper, 55°F; eggplant, 60°F.

Germination time at 70°F[2]	Germination to potting up	Potting up to garden[3]	Nighttime temperature at transplant[4]
4 days	21 days	19 days	50°F
5 days	25 days	14 days	50°F

HERBS COMMONLY GROWN FROM CUTTINGS

Common name *Botanical name*	Production time[1]	Nighttime temperature at transplant[2]
BAY *Laurus nobilis*	60–100 days	55°F
BEE BALM *Monarda* spp.	38 days	55°F
CATNIP *Nepeta cataria*	40 days	50°F
CHAMOMILE, ROMAN *Chamaemelum nobile*	35 days	55°F
CURRY PLANT *Helichrysum italicum*	55 days	50°F
FEVERFEW *Tanacetum* spp.	40 days	55°F
GERANIUM, SCENTED *Pelargonium* spp.	40 days	55°F
HYSSOP *Hyssopus officinalis*	42 days	50°F
LAVENDER *Lavandula* spp.	50 days	55°F
LEMON BALM *Melissa officinalis*	30 days	50°F

Comments

Usually grown as a pot plant

Mildew on foliage can be a problem

Roots quickly

2½–inch cuttings work well

Gray, hairy leaves are fungus-prone; cuttings need less mist or humidity

Especially useful way to save showy flowering varieties

Allow cutting wound to "heal" overnight by placing it in a plastic bag kept in a cool place. Not all varieties root eagerly.

Best way to propagate white- and pink-flowered varieties

Vegetative propagation is a must for named varieties

Easy method when divisions are not possible

HERBS COMMONLY GROWN FROM CUTTINGS

Common name *Botanical name*	Production time[1]	Nighttime temperature at transplant[2]
LEMON VERBENA *Aloysia triphylla*	40 days	55°F
MARJORAM *Origanum majorana*	35 days	55°F
MINT *Mentha* spp.	27 days	55°F
OREGANO *Origanum vulgare* ssp. *hirtum*	35 days	55°F
ROSEMARY *Rosmarinus officinalis*	49 days	55°F
RUE *Ruta graveolens*	53 days	55°F
SAGE *Salvia officinalis*	45 days	55°F
SANTOLINA *Santolina* spp.	60 days	55°F
SAVORY, WINTER *Satureja montana*	50 days	55°F
SOUTHERNWOOD *Artemisia abrotaum*	65 days	55°F

Comments

Guard against mites and white flies on cuttings

Cuttings less likely to develop stem rot

Roots easily in water

Easily rooted and quick to branch

Light-colored, greenish stems root quickly

Propagate handsome named varieties vegetatively. Spring growth roots quickly.

Spring cuttings easiest to root. Best way to produce named varieties with colorful leaves.

Drier rooting conditions protect against disease

Fewer stem-rot problems from cuttings; a good way to preserve variations in flower color.

Seeds not available of this lovely scented herb. Choose new spring growth for easiest rooting.

HERBS COMMONLY GROWN FROM CUTTINGS

Common name *Botanical name*	Production time[1]	Nighttime temperature at transplant[2]
TARRAGON, FRENCH *Artemisia dranunculus*	50 days	55°F
THYME, ENGLISH *Thymus* 'Broad-leaf'	50 days	50°F

[1] Production times are for optimum indoor conditions with root-zone heating and intermittent mist. Production time is measured from the day cuttings are stuck until transplants are garden ready.

[2] Transplanting temperatures are estimates based on average nighttime lows and are related to transplanting common vegetables as follows: broccoli or cabbage, 45°F; tomato or pepper, 55°F; eggplant 60°F.

Comments

Early spring growth roots best; highly susceptible to fungus.

Tender new growth roots quickly; avoid stems in flower.

SPADE WORK

The charm and challenge of successful herb gardening lies in mastering the subtleties. In truth, growing herbs encompasses far more than simply planting seeds, cuttings, or roots. The elements that make for healthy, thriving plants—light, water, soil, nutrients, warmth, luck—don't arrange themselves into tidy recipes. The creatures, large and small, that threaten the wellbeing of herbs don't necessarily wear nametags. Herb gardening requires an ability to assess and balance and intuit that comes as much from the heart as from the head.

Tom DeBaggio is a master of the subtleties. Ask him a simple question, and you can be sure of getting an answer a yard long. Not because he's a roundabout individual, but because there are no true, simple answers in gardening. Gardening can be conducted by formula, but only up to a point.

Through the late 1980s and early 1990s, DeBaggio generously shared his gardening discoveries and insights in a series of columns in The Herb Companion magazine. The column was called "Spade Work," not only in reference to that most basic, earthy tool, but obliquely to the kind of sleuthing that makes gardening an endless adventure. We've selected a few of his more practical essays for inclusion in here, a discursive extension to all the good practical information that has gone before.

THRESHING AROUND
THE HERB GARDEN

Knowing some simple techniques for harvesting seed is more important for herb growers than for other gardeners because seeds, as well as foliage, are important sources of flavor in cooking.

Common herb seeds harvested for kitchen use—lovage, coriander, dill, and fennel—are big and easy to collect. These herbs produce large umbels—broad heads that contain many seeds. Little special equipment is needed to capture these seeds because of their size and the ease with which they separate from the plant. But seeds of these plants rarely ripen all at once, and the umbels tend to shatter, spilling the ripe seed before you can collect it. Harvesting these seeds calls for care and a simple technique to keep them from scattering all over the garden, where they may self-sow plants in unwanted places.

Timing is the key. When a few seeds begin to ripen (signaled by a change from green to gray), I carefully place a small paper bag over each cluster and tie the open end with a piece of string or a wire twist-tie. The seeds continue ripening inside the bag. After two weeks, I lop off the bagged seed-heads, shake the bags to loosen the seeds, and then remove the stems from the bags. This method produces a seed harvest with only a little broken plant material in it. Because the seed is usually ground for use in cooking, I don't bother to remove this aromatic chaff.

Harvesting herb seed for the kitchen is a welcome annual event, but there are other reasons an herb gardener might want to become familiar with seed-collecting techniques. Many herb growers relish the idea of a self-sufficient garden, one in which old plants produce new ones. Others want to save money by collecting their own seed (although surveys report that herb enthusiasts spend less than $10 annually on plants and seeds). And there may always be the unusual plant for which there is no ready source of seeds outside your own garden.

Before I start collecting seeds for planting, I make sure that the seeds will produce plants with the characteristics I desire. There are two problems here. One is that some herbs are sterile, or do not produce plants with the same characteristics as their parents. Many thymes and lavenders, most mints, some oreganos, and tarragon are examples of these. The second problem is unwanted hybridization. For instance, bees may pollinate a green basil with pollen from a purple basil. Offspring grown from the resulting seed may be completely different from either the purple or the green basil. To lessen the chances of natural hybridization between varieties, it's wise to build a screen-wire cage over the plants from which you want to collect seeds to keep insects from cross-pollinating them.

Once the tiny seeds are ripe and ready to harvest, a set of screens removes much of the tedium of cleaning them. Six separate screens, ranging from a number 8 (64 openings per square inch) to a number 30 (900 openings per square inch), will handle most of the seed sizes produced by herb plants. I mount these foot-square screens on narrow wooden frames to give them rigidity and to allow different sizes to be stacked over one another. With a double- or triple-decker arrangement, I can mash the seed heads on the top screen to catch the large trash while the seeds sift down to tile lower screens. I blow away any remaining chaff.

I store ripe seed heads in large paper bags to process in the fall when there aren't so many garden chores. This method allows me to collect all my seeds and then confine the mess of seed cleaning to one time and place. For my tiny-leaved Greek basil (about 20,000 seeds per ounce), I use a number 12 screen on top and a number 16 screen in the middle, and catch the seed on a number 20 screen. For sage (about 3,400 per ounce) and fennel (about 8,000 per ounce), I mount a number 8 over a number 12. An extremely fine number 30 screen is handy for oregano and thyme (about 200,000 and 100,000 seeds per ounce, respectively).

After the seed is separated, I store it in breathable material—cloth sacks or paper envelopes. I try to keep the seed in a place where the temperature and humidity, when added together, don't equal more than 100—a handy rule of thumb for maintaining viability.

Threshing around in the herb garden not only supplies an abundance of seeds for the kitchen and next year's garden, it brings all emotional glow of fulfillment and self-sufficiency. Not to mention an aroma that provides a quintessential herbal experience.

August/September 1990

IN A COLD FRAME OF MIND

When fall brings a nip to the air, I get into a cold frame of mind. It's not depressing in the least, and it doesn't make me any more acerbic than normal. It's my way of greeting winter with a warm buffer around some of my favorite herb plants.

A cold frame may sound like a close relative to an icebox, but the two are as different as the winters in Minnesota and Florida. A cold frame is a miniature greenhouse which requires only modest skill and investment to build, and it can, in temperate climates, become the most valuable tool in the herb garden. A good cold frame keeps the temperature inside it 15 to 20 degrees higher than that outside without any heat other than the sun's rays. This, along with its size and portability, makes a cold frame indispensable for early seed starting and preparing seedlings for spring transplanting. In many areas of the country, protection in a cold frame can mean the difference between life and death for many herb plants. More important, this simple, easy-to-build device can extend the season for fresh herbs and, in many cases, deliver them to the table all winter without the clutter of pots on the windowsill.

Some of the best herbs to grow in a cold frame are often miserly producers during warmer weather. Chervil, dill, coriander, and parsley can become monsters under the long, cool growing conditions provided by a cold frame. Other herbs particularly suited as cold-frame crops are sorrel, rosemary, oregano, thyme, and sweet marjoram, and potherbs such as rucola (arugula) and radicchio.

Over the years, I've had many styles and sizes of cold frames. The simplest was made from old window sashes and treated 2-by-8 lumber. The wooden frame, sized to the width of the sashes, was about 6 feet from east to west and 4 feet from north to south. I placed the 16-inch-high back against a fence to the north; the front sloped to 8 inches, so that the window sashes would slough off rain and snow and the glass faced south to capture the winter sun. I removed 6 inches of earth inside the frame, backfilled with 3 inches of crushed stone, and lined the earthen edge with bricks to hold heat for the potted plants I placed in it. For added heat retention, I could have stationed water bottles painted black around the inside perimeter of the frame.

Later, I built a more ambitious cold frame to cover a raised garden bed. This one was designed on the theory that it's easier to take the cold frame to the plants than to take the plants to the cold frame. It was my favorite for portability because it could be rolled up and put away at the end of the winter. To make it, I punched 2-foot lengths of electrical conduit into the ground along opposite edges of the herb bed, 4 feet apart. Into each pair of opposite pipes I shoved the ends of a 10-foot length of 1/2-inch, flexible plastic water pipe. These pipes arched over the bed, forming a framework that supported a 12-foot-wide sheet of clear, 6-mil polyethylene. One side of the plastic was folded and stapled to the wooden side of the raised bed with heavy-duty staples. The ends and the remaining side were held down by cinder blocks to permit easy opening on warm days.

Right now, I'm dreaming of a deluxe, roomy cold frame in which I can store my collection of tender rosemary and lavender plants this winter. The frame will be rigid, made of factory-bent square steel hoops. The cold frame made by connecting these hoops with pieces of straight steel is to be hinged with an ingenious T made of two pieces of welded pipe. The side rail will run through the horizontal piece of the T, while the vertical piece will slip over a ground stake to make a hinge. The entire top will lift for access and ventilation. The frame is to be covered with a double layer of clear polyethylene inflated by a small fan similar to those used in auto heaters. The gravel bed inside the frame will be heated by circulating hot water. At one end will be a thermostatically triggered exhaust fan, at the other a louvered opening through which fresh air will be pulled in.

Cultivating plants successfully in a cold frame requires careful heat control. Air can heat up fast inside, cooking the plants you're trying to keep from freezing. Siting your cold frame close to the house makes tending it easier. To limit fungus diseases spawned by high humidity, ventilate regularly and increase air movement. If necessary, apply liquid garden sulfur to kill mildew.

The problems of cold frame cultivation are few compared to the fun it provides. So when a cold frame of mind sets in, surrender to it and enjoy the pleasures of your herb garden all winter. It's one of the best ways for an herb gardener to retain a pleasant demeanor during piercing cold weather and at the same time produce some exceptional crops.

October/November 1990

READING HERB LEAVES

Nearly everybody recognizes that a droopy plant needs water. Wilting is an example of the way plants send visual messages about their health. It's as if they were talking to you.

Because people and plants don't speak the same language, misinterpretation of the plant's message is easy. For instance, when rosemary leaves turn black or brown and drop, it's commonly believed to signal a lack of humidity in the air. This prompts the oft-heard advice to mist the plants. What makes rosemary leaves turn color and drop has to do with moisture, all right—but not around the leaves. It's too much water around the roots that is making them rot.

Even a wallflower at a high school dance knows that one glance does not a conversation make; it takes more than a wink and a hello to create meaningful dialog. And just as our own language is tangled with ambiguity, so may an herb's messages have several translations. For the conversation to be meaningful, you need to know the optimum cultural requirements of the herb, including light, temperature, fertility, water, and soil pH. It's also useful to know what insects and diseases typically attack it. A good dictionary of this language is not easy to find; many herb books give pests and diseases a quick brushoff, as if such problems didn't exist.

I held a conversation with four basils the other day. I began with a general examination which led to questions that probed the vital signs. I could see from ten yards away that the basils had been pitifully neglected. The plants were stunted; the leaves were limp and yellow-ish; days of hot sun had caked and split the soil. It was easy to see that the plants were too dry and needed water. But what had caused the lack of growth and the anemic leaf color?

You need a basic vocabulary to have a téte-á-téte with a basil. You need to know, for instance, that basil is a nitrogen lover and that yellowed leaves and failure to grow might be its way of telling you it is fertilizer-starved. So I mixed up some 20-10-20 liquid fertilizer (20 percent nitrogen, 10 percent phosphorus, and 20 percent potash) and applied it—irrigation and essential nutrients for growth, all at once. In a matter of hours the plants were standing upright. A week later, the color had returned to their leaves and the plants were growing vigorously.

Reading herb leaves isn't always so simple; it can be tricky. With that in mind, here are some typical herb messages with their translations and appropriate responses.

Message: Dead leaves hanging on branches low to the soil.

Translation: Suspect fungus disease.

Response: The disease spreads with moisture. Remove infected dead, yellowing, and damaged foliage. Increase air circulation within and around the plant by judicious pruning and increased spacing. Add a mulch of white plastic or sand to reflect heat into the plant to help keep leaves dry. Liquid garden sulfur sprays kill some types of fungus.

Message: Sudden collapse or wilting of the plant when adequate irrigation is available.

Translation: Suspect *Phytophthora*, a soil disease that attacks many herbs native to the Mediterranean basin, causing roots to rot.

Response: Do not replant susceptible species in the same spot. Improve soil drainage by adding compost or other humus-rich amendments.

Message: Pinhead-size discolorations on leaves, wiggly discoloration through leaf surfaces, ragged holes in leaves or leaf-margins.

Translation: The critters—spider mites, leaf miners, and slugs—are getting your herbs before you do.

Response: Repeated, forceful sprays of water under leaves will dislodge spider mites; spraying with insecticidal soap will kill them. Cover spring and fall with light, spun-bonded poly cover to keep egg-laying leaf miners from leaves. Night-foraging slugs live under stones and next to fence posts near plants. Seek them out and destroy: scatter diatomaceous earth around the bases of plants, or place 4-inch-wide copper flashing around plants.

Message: Poor growth, yellowing leaves, drying growing tips.

Translation: After discounting pH imbalance, poor drainage, or lack of nutrients, consider microscopic soil insects called nematodes. They burrow into roots, causing raised nodes and interfering with nutrient uptake.

Response: Soil enriched with grass clippings helps destroy nematodes. Failing all else, turn to container gardening. A good growing medium is one containing peat moss and perlite in equal parts.

To grow healthy, vigorous herb plants, the gardener needs to practice the art of observation. It's an important form of communication in the garden.

June/July 1990

WHEN UGLY MAKES BEAUTY

Not long ago, I spent a pleasant summer afternoon chatting with another gardener about pruning herbs. The theme of the conversation developed quickly: many of life's experiences are humbling, but few are more so than herb gardening. Before we got totally mired in pessimistic blather, I offered this axiom: "When an herb is looking gorgeous," I said, "make it ugly." In other words, render your beautiful, lush herbs into ugly stubble so that they may better persevere.

This seemingly perverse rule makes it possible to cultivate well-mannered, healthy herbs in climates that have humid, hot, dewy summers—perfect conditions for rapid fungus growth. If that describes your climate, too, you'll need to give butch haircuts to your fungus-susceptible herbs—culinary sages, whether variegated, small or large leaved; semiupright thymes that make thick mounds; French tarragon that bends under its own weight; thickly branched santolina; tangled oregano; heavy stands of thick mints; floppy lavender; unruly rosemary; wildly spreading lambs'-ears; and others that embrace the earth too closely.

In my Virginia garden, I perform the first harvest-cum-tonsorial surgery about July 4. This may be the nation's celebration of independence from Britain, but it's also the beginning of the fungus season. Fungus grows in a moist atmosphere and spreads on droplets of water. It thrives on the dead leaves and other interior debris of seemingly healthy, bushy plants, unseen to the garden stroller. Then one day, often after a summer shower, darkened, fungus-ridden foliage suddenly shows through the green canopy that has hidden it.

If the disease has not progressed too far, I have found that a quick cleanup and pruning (the horticultural equivalent of a shave and a haircut) does the trick. Once the dead foliage is removed and the plant is opened to drying air and sunlight, the need for more severe prophylactic treatment such as spraying with fungicides is lessened.

This polite summer surgery is definitely not a wack-wack affair. I carefully remove one-third to one-half of every stem. Sharp stainless steel scissors are handy for this, but my favorite tool is a small, straight-bladed, light-duty pruner. The remaining stems, usually covered with soggy dead foliage, are thoroughly cleaned, and debris on the ground is removed. I take care to top the plant into a pleasant geometric shape. I may decide to remove extremely low branches at the plant's base to permit air to circulate under the plant. Sand, small stones, or other light-colored, nonabsorbent material make a good mulch because they reflect heat and light into the plant and thus help to keep the interior dry.

This adroit scalping not only eliminates fungus, it also encourages new, vigorous growth that produces a bountiful late summer harvest.

Careful pruning in the spring, long before fungus season arrives, can help control summer disease problems, too. Spring is when I create what a visiting wag once referred to as a stick garden. I go through this uglification process on my budding herbs to rejuvenate them and control their growth to fit the space available. (When one plant grows faster and larger, its neighbor may suffer from disease fostered by lack of air and light.)

I begin the spring pruning ritual when small nodules begin to swell along herb stems. These infantile branches will burst into growth after pruning. I single out thyme, sage, lavender, rosemary, and other woody perennials for these spring rites. I look among the sprouting woody branches carefully for winter damage and remove dead branches and stems. As in the summer to come, I try to shorten the branches of these budding herbs by one-third to one-half their length. If they're in pots that have been indoors all winter, I may remove a little more. Inside or out, I leave some greenery on the branches or make sure there are plenty of growth nodules remaining on bare stems.

Branching will occur only at the ends of the stems if they are not cut as spring growth commences, and the lower part of the plant will quickly become woody and barren of foliage.

For me, pruning herbs is separate and apart from harvesting their foliage for the kitchen (though these two activities often overlap). Pruning is so central to their future health and productivity that I approach the process with fervor because I know that what may appear to be radical surgery will produce better branching, improved vigor, and healthy plants.

August/September 1991

HERB COMMANDMENTS

Etiquette. Rules of behavior. The process of natural selection in the garden center. These aren't the spring thoughts on which I normally dwell, and herb gardening shouldn't ordinarily be constrained by them. On the other hand, the moralist in me has never hesitated to impose all manner of rules on others. So it's in that spirit that I hand down these Commandments of Herb Buying.

I. When you go to purchase your herbs, look around the place that you've walked into. It's probably a greenhouse. But is it neat and orderly? Are there lots of plants around? A wide selection? All the plants identified with clearly printed labels? Good. Neatness and cleanliness are signs that the owner cares about details. Maybe there are some good, healthy plants here. And go to a specialist if possible. A greenhouse or garden center that deals only in herbs, or that has a sizable herb department, is likely to have fresher stock and more knowledgeable personnel.

II. Take off your dark glasses. How can you judge the subtleties of leaf color that will convey the health and vigor of the plant with those shades over your eyes? Look for vigor and bushiness. Look for roots hanging out of the drainage holes. Oh, boy, you say, I've heard that's a bad sign, not a good one. Rootbound—a no-no. But are you going to keep the little thing in that pot, or plant it in your garden? Think about it.

Bushy plants such as basil, thyme, lavender, hyssop, sage, and rosemary ought to be crazy with branches and new growth, not just long stems with a couple of leaves on top. Even plants that send up lots of shoots from the roots each year, such as mints, lemon balm, catnip, lovage, sorrel, and tarragon, ought to have nice clumps or branching stems. Reject plants with yellowing leaves, leaf-miner trails (especially in oregano, marjoram, and sorrel), pinpoint discoloration on the leaves which indicate spider mite or thrips infestation, larger insects hiding under leaves, or fuzzy growth on dead leaves. Bad stuff, that.

III. If you want to eat the plant, buy it. But don't nibble on it until you've paid for it. Don't pinch it, either. If everybody pinched and tasted, what would be left to sell? The correct way to test the aromatic qualities of an herb is to brush the leaves gently with your hand to release the essential oils, then discreetly sniff the hand that did the brushing or delicately sniff the leaves. Of course, you're not going to stick your nose on the plant! One minute you want to eat all the plants leaf by leaf, the next you want to give everybody your cold!

IV. Now ask a few questions of the proprietor or the Learned Helper. How was the plant grown? From seed or cutting? Annuals are usually grown from seed. Perennials, especially those with variety names, are ordinarily grown from cuttings. For sure, tarragon, all mints, lavenders, rosemaries, oreganos, and thymes should be propagated from cuttings to retain their varietal characteristics. But don't sound like a Grand Inquisitor—be tactful. Ask for cultivation advice. You want to find out if the plants you plan to buy will grow where you plan on growing them. Books are fine for general information, but what you need is information specific to your climate.

V. Try to go on a weekday, especially in late spring. It's too crowded and busy on a weekend. You want time to chat. You want more than the strained civility you're lucky to receive on a weekend. And leave the babies at home if you possibly can.

VI. If you don't have a local herb grower and must buy your plants by mail, this Commandment is for you. Mail-order growers have catalogs. Judge each by its catalog first. Is it orderly, cleanly designed, and easy to use? Are the plant descriptions helpful? Does the catalog contain cultivation information—height, spacing, best growing conditions? Call the compa-

ny and ask how the plants are grown. What size are they? Some companies sell rooted cuttings without pots for $4; others may offer a nicely established plant in a three-inch pot for the same price. A few bucks spent before you write the check may prevent unhappy surprises when the UPS driver arrives with your plants.

Well, keeping your life on track may require Ten Commandments, but selecting herb plants shouldn't be as complicated. Six should do. Picking good herb plants is a little like life, or a ripe melon. You can see its size and shape, and you have an idea of what to expect from past experience. But you never know for sure how it'll taste until you cut it.

April/May 1990

STILL LIVES

Fall and winter have a profound impact on me. The glitter, energy, and warmth of the holidays loosen memories and stir emotions that center on food and gardens, where the deeper meaning of my life is rooted. My thoughts at this time of year often pierce the past and settle on my family, especially my Nonna, a woman I never knew.

Nonna was what everybody called my great-grandmother, Rosa DeBiaggio. In Italian, "nonna" means granny, but she was more than the family matriarch—she was a legend in the kitchen.

The kitchen of Nonna's rustic house in Romans-di-Varmo, in the Friuli region of northeastern Italy, had been in the center of the room on a dirt floor, where the fire burned and the smoke spiraled through a hole in the roof. When you start humble in the kitchen, you stay pure and simple the rest of your life because you learn that freshness and taste surpass style. Her Friuli past followed Nonna when she joined her family in Des Moines, Iowa. When she died in 1937, she left a small, personal legacy in America.

The house my father bought in 1945 had

a kitchen Nonna would have appreciated. It had been a chicken coop before it became a kitchen, and the house grew around it. This put the kitchen where it belonged—close to the center of life. The front of the house looked out on two old, twisted apple trees and a long greensward with the garden in the middle of it. The garden, like the kitchen, was sited appropriately and treated with reverence; its purpose was to grow big, red tomatoes, crisp radishes, scallions, and tender little lettuces with which my father made a salad everybody in the family thought was indigenous to our native Iowa. The production of this simple salad became ritual when my father ceremoniously anointed the fresh greens with crumbled bits of bacon and their hot grease, and a little vinegar. My father called it wilted lettuce salad, and there was never enough of it. Much later, when I read Waverley Root's evocative book, *The Food of Italy*, I learned that this salad was also eaten by the Friulani and called *insalata al lardo*. (How is it that the spirit of a place finds itself reincarnated thousands of miles away?)

In this kitchen that was once a chicken coop, and in the garden on the front lawn, I learned about the importance of food and gardens and memory. My father never announced his intention to teach me about these important things, but on a fall day forty years ago I knew there was something special about to happen in the fading light as I sat on a stool and watched him search his memory for the key to making Nonna's *gnocchi*.

This was before there were books about Italian food written in English; women kept the secrets of this hearty peasant food in their heads. This was also in a time before you could buy good Italian wine in America; what you got was cheap, raw stuff in a big glass bottle wrapped with straw. It's hard to believe that there was ever such a time, but it was so, and that was why my father searched his memory for the motions he had watched Nonna make in the tile kitchen in Des Moines when he was a boy.

My father worked silently. He boiled two baking potatoes, peeled them and mashed them with a fork, and added a cup of flour and a beaten egg. He kneaded the dough that resulted, rolled small pieces of it between his fingers until they were round, and then pressed them gently against a cheese grater and set them aside. When the whole lump of dough had been turned into rough marbles that would collect sauce in their wrinkles, he put water in the big metal spaghetti pot and put it on a lighted burner of the stove. He put the little balls of dough in the pot and turned to look at me with joy and anticipation. "They will float to the top when they are done," he said.

We waited; the water boiled but nothing happened. The balls of dough stuck to the bottom of the pan. His memory had lost something important—the water has to boil vigorously before the *gnocchi* are added to it, a few at a time. My dad looked lost and angry as he scraped the hot pan to loosen his failed *gnocchi*, now a sticky glop of potatoes and flour. He never tried to make *gnocchi* again, and that was an epicurean loss for us; they are inert little dumplings and uninteresting in themselves, but they exist to be graced with fresh herbs. When the *gnocchi* dough is stuffed with rosemary, parsley, and porcini mushrooms, or when they are drenched in creamy sage sauce, the result is something pure and simple and life-giving, one of the true wonders of the culinary world.

Nonna and my dad are gone, but they are part of my invisible matrix. They were not people of any celebrity; they believed in living quiet, still lives. But they tried to keep something precious alive inside themselves and in me—a memory of the past and where they came from. I am often reminded of them when I walk through my herb garden, but memories of them are especially vivid in the fall around Thanksgiving and Christmas, when we eat the food of Italian peasants as if it were holy wafers used to commune with the departed.

For many people, history is a chronicle of past events put down in words and printed in books. For me, history is more fleeting and personal and found in the food, fragrances, and gardens that are windows to memory. This thing we call memory can be random and fitful, but it has a special power of its own—it permits dead souls to animate the present and form rich undercurrents in still lives.

December/January 1991-1992

RESOURCES

I sell no seed, and I don't ship plants. There are hundreds of small enterprises like mine in the United States, and I encourage you to patronize these local establishments because personal contact with herb plants and those who grow them is the best way to determine an herb's suitability for your garden and kitchen. Not everyone is fortunate enough to have excellent local resources, but many mail-order companies now provide hard-to-find seeds and plants. Only a few are listed here.

Readers interested in broadening their herbal education through correspondence and on-site classes will find these listed in Laura Z. Clavio's *Directory of Herbal Education* (Intra-American Specialties, 3014 N 400 West, West Lafayette, Indiana 47906).

HERB SEEDS AND PLANTS

Blossom Farm
34515 Capel
Columbia Station OH 44028
www.blossomfarm.com
Catalog, $1.

Canterbury Farm
Tigard OR 97224
(503) 968-8269
www.canfarms.com

Companion Plants
7247 N. Coolville Ridge Rd
Athens, OH 45701
(740) 592-4643. Catalog, $3.
www.frognet.net/companion_plants/

The Cook's Garden
Box 535
Londonderry VT 05148
(800) 457-9703. Catalog, free.

Dry Creek Herb Farm and Learning Center
13935 Dry Creek Rd
Auburn CA 95602
(503) 878-2441

Garden Medicinals
PO Box 320
Earlysville VA 22936
Catalog, $1.

Garden Trails
5730 W Coal Mine Ave
Littleton CO 80123

Goodwin Creek Gardens
PO Box 83
Williams OR 97544
(800)846-7359. Catalog $1.
www.goodwincreekgardens.com

The Gourmet Gardener
(888) 404 GROW(4769)
E-mail: information@gourmetgardener.com

Gourmet Herbs
3200 Tindall Acres Rd
Kissimmee FL 34744
(407) 957-4847

Grandma's Garden
4N381 Maple Ave
Bensenville IL 60106
www.grandmasgarden.com.
Catalog, $3.

The Herbfarm
32804 Issaquah-Fall City Rd
Fall City WA 98024
(425) 222-7103.

Kettleby Herb Farms
15495 Weston Rd
RR 2
Kettleby ON CANADA
L0G1J0

Ladybug Herbs
943 Richard Woolcutt Rd
Wolcott VT 05680
(802) 888-5940. Catalog, $2.

Le Jarden du Gourmet
Box 75C
St. Johnsbury Ctr. VT 05863
www.herbfarm.com
Catalog, $1 (includes recipes and 4 sample seed packets).

Lewis Mountain Herbs and Everlastings
2345 State Route 247
Manchester, OH 45144
(937) 549-2484. Catalog $1.
www.bright.net/~mtherbs/

Mellinger's
2344 DN W South Range Rd
North Lima OH 44452-9731
(330) 549-3716 (800) 321-7444
www.mellingers.com

Nichols Garden Nursery
1190 S Pacific Highway
Albany OR 97321
(541) 928-9280. Catalog, free.
www.gardennursery.com

No Thyme Productions
8321 SE 61st St
Mercer Island WA 98040
(206) 236-8885
www.nothyme.com
E-mail: info@nothyme.com

Rasland Farm
NC 82 at US 13
Godwin, NC 28344-9712
(910) 567-2705. Catalog, $3.
www.alcasoft.com/rasland/

Richters
357 Highway 47
Goodwood Ontario L0C 1A0
Canada
(905) 640-6677. Catalog, free.
www.richters.com

Sandy Mush Herb Nursery
316 Surrett Cove Rd
Leicester NC 28748-5517
(828) 683-2014. Catalog, $4.

Sunnyboy Gardens, Inc.
3314 Earlysville Rd
Earlysville VA 22936
(804) 974-7350
www.sunnyboygardens.com

Well-Sweep Herb Farm
205 Mt. Bethel Rd
Port Murray NJ 07865
(908) 852-5390. Catalog, $2.

Willhite Seed Inc.
PO Box 23
Poolville TX 76487
(817) 599-8656
E-mail: info@willhiteseed.com

Wrenwood
Rt 4 Bx 8055
Berkeley Springs WV 25422
(304) 258-3071
E-mail: wrenwood@intrepid.net

SEEDS AND SUPPLIES

Johnny's Selected Seeds
Foss Hill Road
Albion ME 04910
(207) 437-4301. Free catalog.
www.johnnyseeds.com

Park Seed Company
Cokesbury Road
Greenwood, SC 27647
(800) 845-3366. The firm's wholesale division has misting equipment and other propagation supplies used by commercial growers. Free catalog.
www.parkwholesale.com

W. Atlee Burpee & Company
Warmister PA 18974
(215) 674-1793. Free catalog

SCENTED GERANIUMS

Davidson-Wilson Greenhouses
RR 2, Box 168
Crawfordsville IN 47933
(765) 364-0556. Free catalog.
www.davidson-wilson.com

SUPPLIES

A. M. Leonard, Inc.
PO Box 816
Piqua OH 45356
(800) 543-8955. Free catalog.
www.amleo.com

Gardener's Supply Company
128 Intervale Rd
Burlington VT 05401
(800) 444-6417. Free catalog.

Charley's Greenhouses & Garden Supplies
17979 State Route 536
Mt Vernon WA 98273
www.charleysgreenhouse.com
(800) 322-4707
fax (800) 233-3078

INDEX

A

aeration
    cuttings and 49
    rooting and 33
angelica
    direct sowing, 7, 9, 12
    from seed, 8, 72–73
    general information 62–63
    light for germination 10
anise hyssop
    direct sowing 9
    from seed 72–73
    general information 62–63
aroma of herbs 2, 4
artemesia, propagation of 34
arugula, 87

B

balm of Gilead, rooting in water 39
bare-root seedlings 38
    transplanting of 49–52
basil
    cross-pollinating of 85
    direct sowing 9
    fertilizing during first year 57
    fungus and 88
    general information 62–63
    nitrogen and 88
    oil glands of 2
    rooting in water 36, 37, 38–39
    seed characteristics 7, 31
    seedling vulnerability 14, 38
    sweet, from seed 72–73
    transplanting temperature 83
    wilt 88–89
bay
    from cuttings 78–79
    general information 62–63
    propagation 46–47
    rooting in water 39
bee balm
    division 34, 37
    from cuttings 78–79

    general information 62–63
borage
    direct sowing 9, 12
    from seed 72–73
    general information 62–63
    light for germination 12
burnet, general information 62–63

C

caraway, direct sowing of 9
catnip
    division 34, 37
    from cuttings 78–79
    from seed 72–73
    general information 62–63
chamomile
    direct sowing of 9
    from cuttings 78–79
    from seed 72–73
    general information 62–63
charts 60–83
chervil
    cold-frame growing 87
    direct sowing of 9
    fertilizing in the first year 57
    from seed 72–73
    general information 62–63
chives
    direct sowing of 9, 17
    division of 34, 35
    from seed 72–73
    general information 64–65
    seed characteristics 7
    clump transplanting 22–29
cold frames
    building, 87
    for hardening off 29, 86–87
    use with cuttings 46
    use with divisions 34
comfrey, general information 64–65
composted bark, in soilless media 17
composted hardwood leaves, use in seed bed 10
composted peanut hulls, in soilless media 17
containers, sterilizing 17
coriander
    cold-frame growing of 87
    direct sowing 9

fertilizing in the first year 57

from seed 72–73

general information 64–65

harvesting seed 85

seed characteristics 7

seed sowing indoors 20–21

    thinning of 19, 22

    transplanting of

    vulnerability of 14

costmary, general information 64–65

covering seeds 17–18

crowns

    division of 4, 34

    natural reproduction of 4

curry plant

    from cuttings 78–79

    general information 64–65

cuttings

    aeration and 41

    herbs grown from 78–79

    rooting in water 34–41

    season for 46

    selecting and preparing 38, 42, 44–49

    spacing 49

    sticking 49

    tending 49–53

D

diatomaceous earth 89

dibble, defined 49

dill

    cold-frame growing 87

    direct sowing 9

    fertilizing in the first year 57

    from seed 72–73

    general information 64–65

    harvesting seed 85

    light for germination 10

    transplanting 52

    vulnerability of 14

direct sowing 11–12

division 34–36

    benefits of 34

    diseases with 36

    methods 35–36

    shock and 36

E

echinacea, germination of 8, 10

essential oil 2–4

F

feeding seedlings 24–25

fennel

    from seed 72–73

    general information 64–65

    harvesting seed 85

fertilizer

    for rooting cuttings 44

    for seedlings 24–25

    trace elements and 18

    use in seedbed 10, 12

    use with transplanted cuttings 56–57

feverfew

    from cuttings 78–79

    from seed 74–75

    general information 64–65

    light for germination 10

fish emulsion, for seedlings 25

fluorescent lights, use with

    seed sowing 16–17

    transplanted cuttings 53

foliage disease

    cuttings and 44–46

    seed sowing and 23

fragrance-producing oil 2–4

fungus diseases

    basil and 88

    cold frames and 87

    first year and 57

    pruning and 90

    sowing and 12

    summer 89

G

genetic changes in plants 50–51

geranium, scented

    from cuttings 78–79

    general information 64–65

    'Old Fashioned Rose' 51

    'Rober's Lemon Rose' 51

    rooting in water 37, 39

germination
    seeds and 7–8
    seed spacing and 19–20
    soil preparation for 9–10
germination inhibitor 8
germination rate 7–8
gnocchi, making 92–93
golden lemon thyme, variegation 50–51
growing medium
    containers for 17
    settling, 28
    soilless, creating 18

H

hardening off 29
hardiness 63–71
harvesting herbs 85–86
heat mats 42–43
herbs, buying 91–92
humidity domes 22, 43
hyssop
    from cuttings 78–79
    general information 64–65

I

indole-3-butryic acid, in bay propagation 49
insecticidal soap, 88

L

lady's mantle, general information 64–65
lambs' ears
    general information 66–67
    pruning 90
lavandin, general information 66–67
Lavandula dentata 31
lavender
    from cuttings 46, 78–79
    general information 66–67
    oil glands of 3
    propagation of 31
    pruning 90
    rooting in water 36, 39
layering, in natural reproduction 4, 32
leaf discoloration 89
leaf miners 89

lemon balm
    direct sowing 9
    dividing 37
    feeding of seedlings 25
    from cuttings 78–79
    from seed 74–75
    general information 66–67
    oil glands of 2
lemon verbena
    from cuttings 80–81
    general information 66–67
    rooting in water 36, 39
lemongrass, division 34, 37
light, for germination 15
lime, garden 10, 18
lovage
    direct sowing 9
    from seed 74–75
    general information 66–67
    harvesting seed 85

M

manure, 10, 56
marjoram
    cold-frame growing 87
    division, 34
    feeding of seedlings 25
    from cuttings 80–81
    from seed 74–75
    general information 66–67
Mexican mint marigold, general information 66–67
mint
    aroma of 4
    division 34, 37
    from cuttings 80–81
    general information 66–67
    pruning 90
    rooting in water 36, 37
    stolons 34
mist
    bay propagation and 47
    rooting cuttings and 42, 50
mulch
    first year and 58
    fungus disease and 88
    layering and 33
myrtle, general information 68–69

N

nasturtiums
    direct sowing of 17
    indoor sowing 21
nematodes 36, 89
nurse leaves, planting depth and 25, 28

O

offsets, division 34
oil, fragrance-producing 2–4
oregano
    cold-frame growing 87
    from cuttings 48, 80–81
    from seed 74–75
    general information 68–69
    Greek 1–3
    Italian oregano
        division 34, 37
        rooting in water 39
        sterility of 8
        pruning 89
        transplanting 57, 74
Osmacote 10, 18

P

parsley
    cold-frame growing of 87
    direct sowing 12, 15, 32
    fertilizing in the first year 57, 84–85
    from seed 8, 32, 74–75
    general information 68–69
patchouli 37
pennyroyal seedlings 5
peppermint, sterility of 8
perlite, in soilless media 18
pH levels of soil 10, 89
Phytophthora 89
pineapple sage, rooting in water 36
Pro-Mix BX, for rooting cuttings 42
propagating bay 46–47
pruning 53, 56, 57, 90–91

R

rhizomes, divison 34

root rot 12, 88, 89
root-zone heat
    bay propagation and 46–47
    temperatures for cuttings 42, 46
roots
    division 34
reproduction by 4, 27, 57
rooting
    aeration and 19, 41
    inducing 33
    wounding and 33, 36–37, 38
rooting cuttings
    fertilizer and 44, 53
    growing medium and 42
    in water 37–49
    procedure 37–41
    season for 39
    transplanting 40, 53
    perlite and 42
    sphagnum peat and 42
    vermiculite and 42
rooting hormone 45, 49
rooting medium, desired characteristics 42
rooting stem cuttings 36–53
rosemary
    cold-frame growing 87
    from cuttings 80–81
    general information 68–69
    'Golden Rain' 50–51
propagation of 50, 51
pruning 90
    rooting in water 37, 39
    root rot and 88
    row covers, 13–14
rucola 87
rue
    from cuttings 80–81
    general information 68–69

S

sage
    aroma of 4
    direct sowing 9
    from cuttings 80–81
    from seed 74–75
    general information 68–69
    pruning 89
    rooting in water 37, 39

santolina
    from cuttings 80–81
    general information 68–69
    pruning 89
savory
    general information 68–69
    from seed 74–75
    summer 23
    winter
        from cutting 80–81
        layering 59
seed
    collecting 85–86
    complexity of 7
    covering for germination 12, 72–77
    depth to sow 12
    direct sowing 12
    germination
    guidelines 72–77
soil temperatures and 8
    herbs grown from 72–77
    light for germination 12
slow-growing perennials 15, 54
sowing indoors 17–25
sowing outdoors 9–12
storing 8, 86
seedbed preparation 9–10
seedlings
    bare-root 14, 25
    feeding of 24–25
    leaf types 25
    root system, handling 25–28
stem elongation 25
    transplanting 13–14, 25–29
    vulnerability of 14
    watering 23–24
selecting and preparing cuttings 44–46
shock
    division and 36
    transplanting and 28, 36
'Silver King' artemisia, division 34, 37
simple rooting environments 43
slugs
    controlling 58, 88
    seedlings and 14
soil
    amendments 10, 56
    preparation for germination 9–10
    temperatures for germination 8, 9, 10

testing 10
    treating for rooting 33
soilless growing medium 17, 19, 42
    covering seeds with 17–18
    germination and 17
    recipe for 18
sorrel
    cold-frame growing 87
    direct sowing 9
    division 34, 37
    general information 68–69
    from seed 74–75
southernwood
    from cuttings 80–81
    general information 68–69
sowing seed
    amount 19, 22
    covering and 12, 17, 19, 22, 72–77
    fluorescent lights and 16
    humidity domes and 22, 43
    indoors 17–22
    moisture and 12
    outdoors 9–12
    overwatering and 12
    root rot and 12
    season and 10
    spacing and 19–20
    technique 10, 12, 15
    temperature and 15
    watering 12
sphagnum peat
    for seed germination 8
    in seedbed 10
    in soilless media 18
spider mites, 89
sterile herbs, propagation of 31–32
sterilizing containers 17
stolons 34
sweet Annie, aroma of 4
sweet cicely, germination of 8
sweet woodruff, division 34, 37

T

tansy, general information 70–71
tarragon
    division 34, 37
    French
        general information 70–71

pruning 89
rooting in water 39
sterility of 8
from cuttings 82–83
tending cuttings 49–53
tending transplants 55–56
thyme
aroma of 4
cold-frame growing 87
English 8, 70
feeding seedlings of 25
from cuttings 82–83
from seed 76–77
general information 70–71
layering 32
rooting in water 39
trace elements, fertilizers and 42
transplanting
bare-root cuttings 41
clump 22–29
condition of seedlings for 25, 28–29
cuttings 40, 41, 53
depth for 28, 56
environment control and 28, 29
fertilizing and 29, 53, 56
indoor-grown seedlings 25–29
outdoor-grown seedlings 13–14
rooted cuttings 40, 41
seedlings into pots 27–29
seedlings, spacing of 28
temperatures for 55, 72–83
timing of, 25, 55–56
to garden 55–56

watering and 28, 56
weather and 13, 56

U

umbrellas for seedlings 13

V

variegated foliage, propagation of 31
varietal selection 50–51
vegetative propagation 31–53

W

water, sowing and 12
watering during the first year 56
weeding during the first year 57–58
woody-stemmed herbs, layering 43
wormwood
from seed 76–77
general information 70–71
light for germination 10
wounding
in bay propagation 46–47
rooting in water 38
to accelerate rooting 33

Y

yarrow, general information 70–71